AUGUST LIVSHITZ

TEST YOUR CHESS IQ

Grandmaster Challenge

EVERYMAN CHESS

www.everymanchess.com

First published in 1981 by Pergammon Press (Cadogan Chess)

This edition Published by Gloucester Publishers Ltd in 1993
Copyright © 1981 August Livshitz
English Translation Copyright © 1993 Ken Neat

British Library Cataloguing-in-Publication Data

A catalogue record for this book is available from the British Library.

ISBN: 978-1-857744-002-7

Distributed in North America by National Book Network,
15200 NBN Way, Blue Ridge Summit, PA 17214. Ph: 717.794.3800

Distributed in Europe by Central Books Ltd.,
50 Freshwater Road, Chadwell Heath, London, RM8 1RX Ph: 44(0)845 458 9911

All other sales enquiries should be directed to Everyman Chess:
Email: info@everymanchess.com; Website www.Everymanchess.com

Everyman is the registered trademark of Random House Inc. and is used in this work under license from Random House Inc.

EVERYMAN CHESS SERIES
Chief Advisor: Byron Jacobs
Cover Design: Horacio Monteverde
Printed and bound in the UK by TJ International Ltd, Padstow, Cornwall.

CONTENTS

Introduction vii

Combinational Themes:

Double Attack 1
Discovered Attack 3
Discovered Check 5
Pin 7
Diversion 11
Decoy 19
Interference 23
Defence-elimination 25
Square-vacation 29
Line-opening 31
Utilization of open files 41
Diagonal-opening 43
Utilization of open diagonals 51
Smothered mate 53
Blocking 55
X-ray 55
Overloading 55
Exploiting a back rank weakness 59
Weakness of the second rank 65
Intermediate move 67
Creation and utilization of passed pawns 67
Breakthrough 75
Simplifying combinations 77
Drawing combinations 81
Traps 85
Attack on the kingside castled position 89
Attack on the king caught in the centre 97
Destructive combinations 103

Index of Players 127

CONTENTS

Introduction ... vii

Combinational Themes

Double Attack ... 1
Discovered Attack ... 5
Discovered Check ... 11
Pin ... 15
Diversion ... 19
Decoy ... 23
Interference ...
Defence elimination ...
Square vacation ... 29
Line-opening ... 31
Utilization of open files ... 41
Diagonal-opening ...
Utilization of open diagonals ... 51
Smothered mate ... 55
Blocking ... 55
X-ray ... 59
Overloading ... 59
Exploiting a back rank weakness ...
Weakness of the second rank ... 65
Intermediate move ... 67
Creation and utilization of passed pawns ...
Breakthrough ... 75
Simplifying combinations ... 77
Drawing combinations ... 81
Traps ... 85
Attack on the king-side castled position ... 89
Attack on the king-side castled position ... 97
Destructive combinations ... 105

Index of Players ... 127

INTRODUCTION

Dear Reader! Before you is our third book on chess combinations. We should straight away make the reservation that, if you are unacquainted with Books 1 and 2, you will find it difficult on your own to cope with the tests in this book.

The arrangement and the tests in this book differ somewhat from those in Books 1 and 2. These tests are aimed primarily at players of master strength, or those approaching it. In Russia this corresponds to the grades of Candidate Master and Master of Sport (about 200+ on the BCF scale, or 2200+ on the Elo scale). The system offered was tested for more than ten years with the youth team of the Russian Republic, which in its time included the former World Champion Anatoly Karpov, grandmasters Balashov, Rashkovsky, Sveshnikov, Timoshchenko and Tseshkovsky, and many others who subsequently became well-known players.

The essence of the system is as follows. The evaluation of each test is worked out on a 5-point scale. The highest score of 5 is awarded for a correct solution, including all the most important variations. If the solver indicates a subtlety not mentioned in the solution, his score may be increased by 1 point. Often the solver will find a second path, apart from the author's, one which is also correct. In this case the score should again be 5 points. A score of 4 is awarded for a correct but incomplete solution. For example, an important defensive resource may have been omitted. If the start is indicated correctly, but the essential "point" is missed, a score of 3 is given. When a correct start is made, but then a bad oversight is committed, a score of 2 is awarded. If only the first move is given correctly, the solver receives 1 point. If no solution is given, or if it is a completely incorrect one, no points are awarded.

We have determined a guiding time for each position, depending upon the degree of difficulty. The total time allotted to one test should be not less than two hours, but also not more than three. While in the previous books the time allotted to a test was considerably less, here, taking account of the complexity and serious nature of the examples, we consider the indicated time to be the most reasonable.

In solving the examples in this book, you should not, as in the previous books, put the accent on one definite theme, but should select for yourself 8-12 examples beforehand, alternating them from the various themes. And here we should draw your attention to the fact that all answers should be written down, and should be checked with the correct solutions only after you have solved all the positions in the projected test. Basing yourself upon the time planned, choose positions by alternating difficult ones with less difficult ones. As in Books 1 and 2, you should award yourself bonus or penalty time points, at the rate of one point per five minute difference from the suggested total time.

Your Chess IQ

There are altogether 378 positions in this book, so that a 100% solution can earn you a total of 1890 points. With time bonuses it is possible, of course, to earn a score in excess of 100%. On the basis of the solutions to a small sample of positions submitted by a range of volunteers, we suggest the following "Chess IQ" table:

Percentage score	Actual score	BCF Rating	Elo Rating
120	2270	230	2440
110	2080	215	2320
100	1890	200	2200
90	1700	185	2080
80	1510	170	1960
70	1320	155	1840
60	1130	140	1720

You will no doubt be keen to observe your progress as you make your way through the book, and we suggest that you keep a record of your scores and comments. When you have completed all of the positions, or at least a significant number, we would be pleased to hear from you.

Theme: "Double Attack" (Nos. 1-10)

1. White to play (8 mins.)   **2.** White to play (10 mins.)

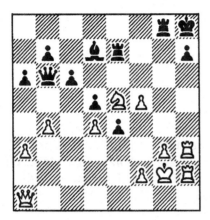 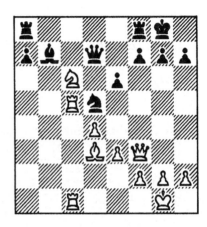

3. White to play (8 mins.)   **4.** Black to play (7 mins.)

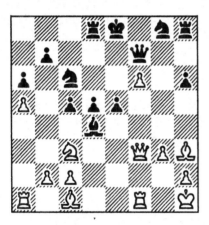 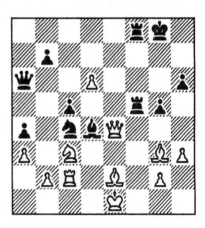

5. White to play (8 mins.)   **6.** Black to play (12 mins.)

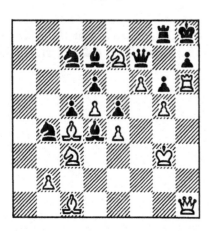 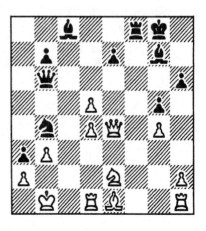

SOLUTIONS TO POSITIONS 1-6

1. **Ebralidze-Lubensky, Tbilisi, 1949**
   1 ♖xh7+!! ♖xh7 2 ♖xh7+ ♔xh7 3 ♕h1+ ♔g7 4 f6+! ♔xf6 5 ♘xd7+ Black resigns.

2. **Honfi-Szabadi, Budapest, 1963**
   1 ♗xh7+!! ♔xh7 2 ♕h3+ ♔g8 3 ♖xd5 ♗xc6 (after *3...♕c7 or 3...♕e8 White wins by 4 ♖h5, e.g. 3...♕c7 4 ♖h5 g6 5 ♖h8+ ♔g7 6 ♖h7+ ♔g8 - or 6...♔f6 7 ♕f3+ ♔g5 8 h4 mate - 7 ♕h6 and wins, or 3...♕e8 4 ♖h5 f6 5 ♖h8+ ♔f7 6 ♕h5+)* 4 ♖xd7 ♗xd7 5 ♕f3 Black resigns.

3. **Minev-Pelinkov, Sofia, 1956**
   1 ♘xd5!! ♕xd5 (bad is *1...♖xd5 2 ♗e6! ♕xe6 3 f7+ ♔f8 4 fxg8=♕+ ♔xg8 5 ♕f8+ ♔h7 6 ♖f7+)* 2 f7+ ♔f8 3 fxg8=♕+ ♔xg8 4 ♕xd5+ ♖xd5 5 ♗e6+ Black resigns.

4. **Novokhatsky-Levi, Volgograd, 1971**
   1...♖f1+!! 2 ♗xf1 ♖xf1+ 3 ♔xf1 ♘d2+ 4 ♔e1 ♘xe4 5 ♘xe4 ♕d3!! and Black won. The finish was 6 ♖e2 ♕b1+ 7 ♔d2 ♕xb2+ 8 ♔d1 ♕b3+ 9 ♔d2 c4 10 d7 ♗b6 11 ♗d6 ♕d3+ 12 ♔e1 c3, and White resigned.

5. **Szabo-Nikitin, Corr., 1964**
   1 ♖xh7+!! ♕xh7 2 f7! ♖d8 (*2...♖f8 fails to 3 ♘xg6+, 4 ♕xh7+ and 5 ♘xf8+*) 3 ♘xg6+ ♔g7 4 f8=♕+ ♖xf8 5 ♕xh7+ ♔xh7 6 ♘xf8+ Black resigns.

6. **Tolush-Kopylov, Leningrad, 1954**
   1...♗xg4!! 2 ♗xb4 (on *2 ♕xg4 there follows 2...♕g6+ 3 ♔a1 ♘c2+ 4 ♔b1 ♘xd4+ 5 ♔a1 ♘c2+ 6 ♔b1 ♘b4+)* 2...♗f5 3 ♕xf5 ♖xf5 4 ♗xa3 ♕a6 5 ♘g3 ♖f2 6 ♘e4 ♖f4 White resigns.

7. Black to play (15 mins.)

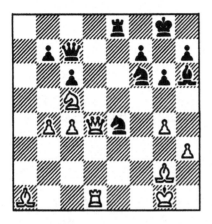

8. White to play (10 mins.)

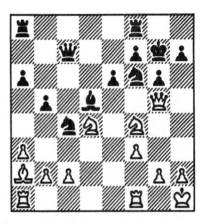

9. Black to play (5 mins.)

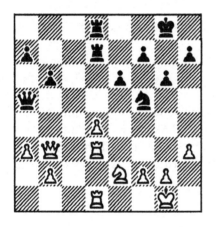

10. Black to play (16 mins.)

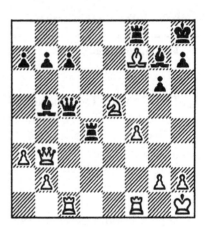

Theme: "Discovered Attack" (Nos.11-16)

11. White to play (7 mins.)

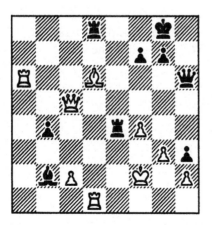

12. White to play (10 mins.)

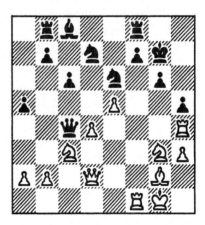

SOLUTIONS TO POSITIONS 7-12

7. **Chechelian-Baikov, Moscow, 1974**
    1...♘g3! 2 ♕d6 (on *2 ♕xf6* there follows *2...♗e3+!*) 2...♖e1+! 3 ♔f2 ♖f1+!! 4 ♗xf1 ♘fe4+ 5 ♔f3 ♘xd6 6 ♗e5 ♘xf1 7 ♘e4 ♘d2+ 8 ♖xd2 ♘xe4 White resigns.

8. **Peretz-Szeles, Budapest, 1968**
    1 ♘f5+!! exf5 (if *1...♔g8 2 ♕xf6 gxf5 3 ♘h5 ♕e5 4 ♕h6* or *4 ♗xc4*) 2 ♕xf6+ ♔xf6 3 ♘xd5+ ♔e5 4 ♘xc7 ♖a7 5 ♖fe1+ ♔d6 6 ♘e8+ Black resigns.

9. **Kholmov-Gligoric, Moscow, 1947**
    1...♘xd4! 2 ♘xd4 ♖xd4 3 ♖xd4 ♖xd4 4 ♖xd4 ♕e1+ 5 ♔h2 ♕e5+ 6 ♕g3 ♕xd4, and Black won.

10. **Tseshkovsky-Tseitlin, Novosibirsk, 1971**
    1...♖xf4!! 2 ♘xg6+ (White thought that this move would win for him, but...) 2...hxg6 3 ♕h3+ ♕h5 4 ♕xh5+ gxh5 5 ♖xf4 ♗h6! (this move White had not foreseen) 6 ♖c5 (if *6 ♖cf1 ♗xf4 7 ♖xf4 ♗e8!*) 6...♗xf4 7 ♖xh5+ ♗h6! 8 ♖xb5 ♖xf7, and Black won. The finish was 9 g4 ♗e3 10 ♖xb7 ♗b6 White resigns.

11. **Werle-Lundin, Sweden, 1969**
    1 ♗e5!! ♕xa6 (or *1...♖e2+ 2 ♔f3! ♕h5+ 3 g4!*) 2 ♖xd8+ ♔h7 3 ♖h8+! ♔g6 (*3...♔xh8 4 ♕f8+ and 5 ♕xg7+*) 4 f5+! ♔g5 5 ♕e7+ f6 6 ♕xg7+ Black resigns.

12. **Markland-Hort, Hastings 1970/71**
    1 ♗d5!! cxd5 (the game in fact went *1...♕xf1+ 2 ♔xf1 cxd5 3 ♘xd5 b6 4 ♘f4 ♘xf4 5 ♕xf4 ♗a6+ 6 ♔g1 ♗d3 7 ♕g5 ♔h8 8 ♕h6+*, and Black resigned) 2 ♘xh5+! gxh5 3 ♕g2+ ♔h6 4 ♖f5 ♘g7 5 ♕xg7+!! and White wins.

13. White to play (10 mins.)

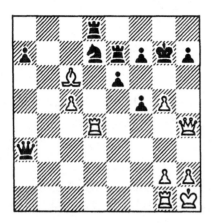

14. White to play (8 mins.)

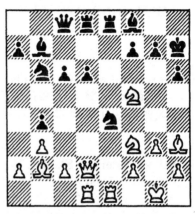

15. White to play (10 mins.)

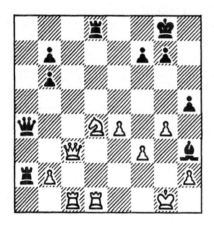

16. Black to play (15 mins.)

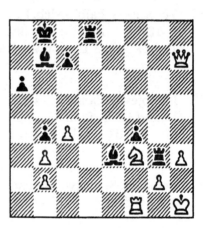

Theme: "Discovered Check" (Nos. 17-22)

17. White to play (8 mins.)

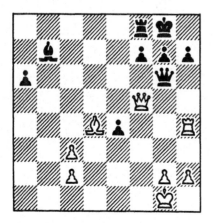

18. White to play (10 mins.)

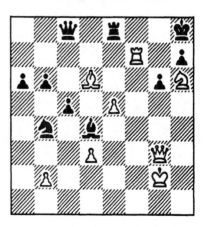

SOLUTIONS TO POSITIONS 13-18

13. **Bronstein-Patzl, Krems, 1967**
     1 g6! ♛xc5 2 ♕xh7+ ♔f6 3 g7! ♕xd4 4 ♕h8!! ♖g8 (there is nothing better) 5 ♕xg8 ♕g4 6 ♕d8 ♕xg7 7 ♗xd7, and White won.

14. **Bellon-Pederson, Skopje, 1972**
     1 ♖xe4!! ♖xe4 2 ♘xh6! gxh6 (*2... ♕xh3 3 ♘g5+*, while if *2... ♕c7*, then again *3 ♘g5+*) 3 ♖xc8 ♗xc8 4 ♘g5+! hxg5 5 ♕xg5 ♖de8 6 ♕h5+ Black resigns (on *6... ♗h6* there follows *7 ♕xf7+*).

15. **Vorotnikov-Faibisovich, Leningrad, 1972 (variation)**
     1 ♘f5! ♖xd1+ 2 ♔f2! f6 (if *2... ♖d4 3 ♕c8+ ♔h7 4 ♕f8!*) 3 ♕c8+ ♔h7 4 ♖c7! ♖xb2+ 5 ♔g3 ♖g1+ 6 ♔h4, and White wins.

16. **Ljubojevic-Planinc, Vrsac, 1971**
     1...♗xf3 2 ♖xf3 (if *2 gxf3 ♖d2!*) 2...♖d1+ 3 ♔h2 ♗g1+ 4 ♔h1 ♖g7! 5 ♕h8+ ♔b7 6 ♖d3 ♖e1! 7 g3 ♗d4+ 8 ♔h2 ♖ge7!! White resigns.

17. **Berebora-Somogyi, Hungary, 1985**
     1 ♖g4! ♕xf5 2 ♖xg7+ ♔h8 3 ♖xf7+ ♔g8 4 ♖g7+ ♔h8 5 ♖g6+! Black resigns.

18. **Genin-Cherepkov, Leningrad, 1960 (variation)**
     1 ♕h4!! ♕e6 (*1... ♕d8* fails to *2 ♕xd8 ♖xd8 3 ♗e7!*, and *1... ♕a8+* to *2 ♖f3 ♕b7 3 ♘f7+ ♔g8 4 ♕f6!*) 2 ♖xh7+!! ♔xh7 3 ♘f7+! ♔g7 4 ♕h6+! ♔xf7 5 ♕h7 mate. In the game 1 ♕f4 was played, and Black managed to defend successfully.

19. White to play (5 mins.)

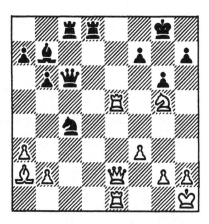

20. White to play (8 mins.)

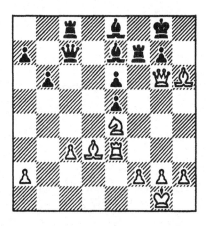

21. Black to play (8 mins.)

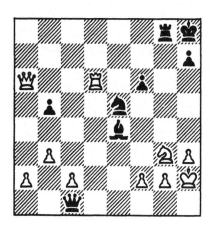

22. White to play (15 mins.)

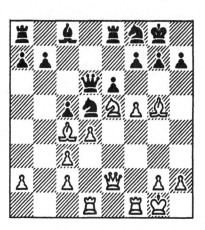

Theme: "Pin" (Nos. 23-30)

23. Black to play (8 mins.)

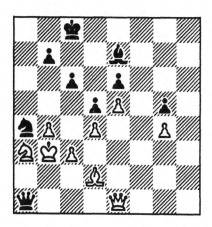

24. Black to play (12 mins.)

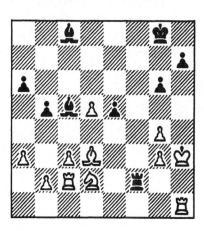

SOLUTIONS TO POSITIONS 19-24

19. Shestoperov-Mikenas, Moscow, 1955

1 ♘xf7!! ♖d2 (the main variation is *1... ♘xe5 2 ♘xe5+*, while on *1... ♔xf7* comes *2 ♖e7+ ♔g8 3 ♕e5*) 2 ♕xd2!! ♘xd2 3 ♘d8+! and wins. The finish was 3...♕c4 4 ♗xc4+ ♘xc4 5 ♖e8+ ♔g7 6 ♘xb7, and Black resigned.

20. Engels-Cardoso, Ribeirao Preto, 1949

1 ♕h7+!! ♔xh7 2 ♘f6+ ♔h8 (or *2... ♔xh6 3 ♖h3+ ♔g5 4 ♖g3+*) 3 ♗xg7+!! ♔xg7 (*3... ♖xg7 4 ♖h3+*) 4 ♖g3+ ♔xf6 (*4... ♔f8 5 ♖g8* mate) 5 ♖g6 mate.

21. Bakulin-Chistyakov, Moscow, 1959

1...♕f1!! 2 ♘xf1 ♖xg2+ 3 ♔h1 ♖xf2+ 4 ♔g1 ♖g2+ 5 ♔h1 ♖g8+ (this wins more quickly than *5... ♖xc2+ 6 ♔g1 ♘f3+ 7 ♔h1 ♘g5+*, as played in the game) 6 ♔h2 ♘f3+ 7 ♔h1 ♖g1 mate.

22. Tal-Chandler, Liverpool, 1974 (from a simultaneous display)

1 ♘xf7!! ♔xf7 2 fxe6+ ♔g8 3 e7 ♘e6 4 dxc5 ♕xc5+ 5 ♔h1 ♘xc3 6 ♖d8!! ♗d7 7 ♕e5!! ♕xe5 (on *7... ♕xc4* there follows *8 ♕xe6+! ♔xe6 9 ♖f8+*) 8 ♖f8+ Black resigns.

23. Bubnov-Terpugov, Moscow, 1961

1...♕b2+ 2 ♔xa4 ♕a2! 3 ♕c1 b5+ 4 ♔a5 ♔b7! White resigns. Against 5...♗d8 mate there is no defence.

24. Mastilovic-Belic, Novi Sad, 1976

1...h5! 2 ♘e4 (or *2 ♗xg6 ♗xg4+ 3 ♔h4 ♗e7 mate*) 2...hxg4+ 3 ♔h4 ♗e7+ 4 ♘g5 ♔g7!! 5 ♗e2 (if *5 ♖xf2 ♔h6* and *6...♗xg5 mate*) 5...♖f8 6 ♗xg4 ♖h8+ White resigns.

25. White to play (5 mins.)

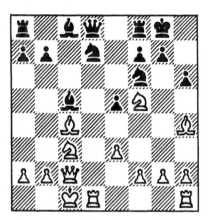

26. White to play (10 mins.)

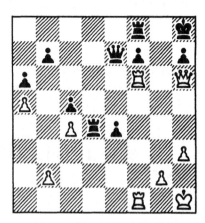

27. Black to play (10 mins.)

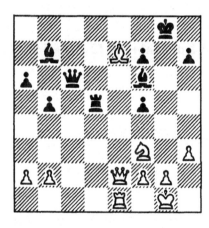

28. Black to play (10 mins.)

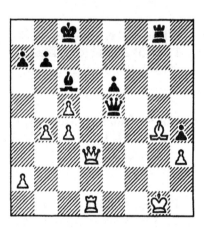

29. White to play (10 mins.)

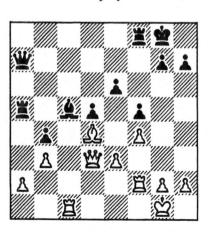

30. Black to play (12 mins.)

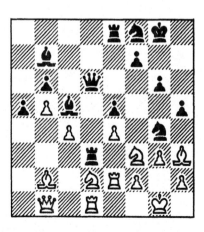

SOLUTIONS TO POSITIONS 25-30

25. **Rudenko-Kogan, Kiev, 1952**
1 ♘xh6+!! gxh6 2 ♖xd7! ♗xd7 3 ♕g6+ ♔h8 4 ♗xf6+ Black resigns.

26. **Karasev-Klaman, Leningrad, 1967**
1 ♖e6! ♕d8 2 ♖g6!! ♖g8 3 ♖xf7 ♖d1+ 4 ♔h2 ♕b8+ 5 g3 ♖d2+ 6 ♔h1 Black resigns.

27. **Sinev-Miagmarsuren, Marianske Lazne, 1962**
1...♖e5! 2 ♕d2 ♖xe7 3 ♕d8+ ♔g7 4 ♖xe7 ♕c1+ 5 ♔h2 ♗xf3 6 gxf3 ♕g5!! White resigns.

28. **White-Duke, Toronto, 1972**
1...♕f5! 2 ♕d4 (or *2 ♔e2 ♗f3!!*) 2...♕f3! 3 ♖d2 ♕h1+ 4 ♔f2 ♖f8+ 5 ♔e3 ♖f3+! White resigns.

29. **Kotov-Kholmov, Moscow, 1971**
1 ♖xc5!! ♖xc5 2 ♖c2 ♖fc8 3 ♕b5!! ♖xc2 4 ♗xa7 ♖xa2 5 ♗c5 h6 6 h4 ♔h7 7 h5 Black resigns.

30. **Planinc-Lombardy, Amsterdam, 1974**
1...♘xf2! 2 ♖xf2 ♖d8! 3 ♔g2 (*3 ♗g2 does not help, since both 3... ♖xf3 and 3...♗xe4!* are threatened) 3...♗xf2 4 ♔xf2 ♕c5+ 5 ♔f1 ♗xe4 6 ♘g5 ♖xd2 7 ♖xd2 ♕xc4+ 8 ♔g1 ♗xb1 9 ♖xd8 ♕e2 White resigns.

Theme: "Diversion" (Nos. 31-56)

31. White to play (5 mins.)

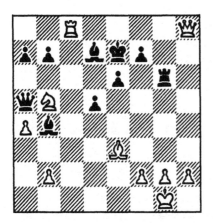

32. Black to play (8 mins.)

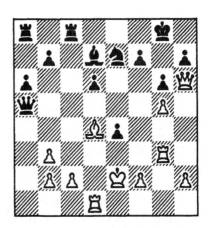

33. White to play (5 mins.)

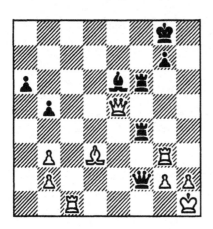

34. Black to play (5 mins.)

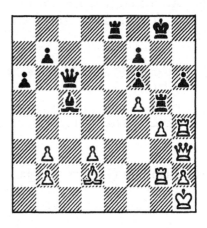

35. White to play (10 mins.)

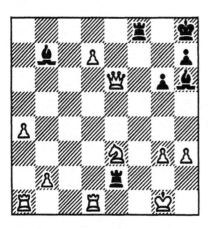

36. Black to play (10 mins.)

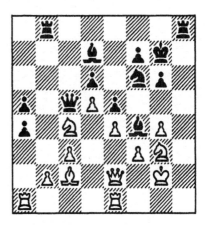

SOLUTIONS TO POSITIONS 31-36

31. Tal-N.N., Riga, 1964 (from a simultaneous display)
1 ♗b6!! ♕xb6 (if *1...axb6 2 ♕d8* mate) 2 ♕h4+ ♖f6 3 ♕xb4+ Black resigns.

32. Panchenko-Kochiev, Riga, 1973
1...♗g4+!! (but not *1... ♘f5?? 2 ♕xh7+!!*) 2 ♖xg4 ♘f5 3 ♕h3 ♖xc2+ 4 ♔f1 ♕b5+ White resigns.

33. Horowitz-N.N., Chicago, 1946 (from a simultaneous display)
1 ♖c8+!! ♗xc8 2 ♕e8+ ♖f8 3 ♖xg7+! ♔xg7 4 ♕g6+ ♔h8 5 ♕h7+ mate.

34. Anen-Lumer, Corr., 1955
1...♗f2!! 2 ♖xh6 ♕c1+!! 3 ♗xc1 ♖e1+ 4 ♖g1 ♖xg1+ mate.

35. Tolush-Mikenas, Moscow, 1951
1 ♕f6+!! (if *1 d8=♕ ♗xe3+ 2 ♕xe3 ♖g2+ 3 ♔h1 ♖d2+*, with a draw by perpetual check) 1... ♖xf6 2 d8=♕+ ♖f8 3 ♕d4+ ♗g7 (or *3...♔g8 4 ♕c4+ and 5 ♕xe2*) 4 ♕d3 ♖ff2 5 ♕xe2 Black resigns (*5... ♖xe2 6 ♖d8+*).

36. Hamilton-Haygarth, England, 1956
1...♘xg4! 2 fxg4 ♗xg4 3 ♕xg4 ♖h2+!! 4 ♔xh2 ♕f2+ 5 ♔h3 (*5 ♔h1 ♗xg3* is no better) 5...Rh8+ White resigns.

37. White to play (12 mins.)

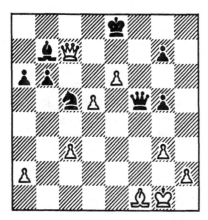

38. Black to play (10 mins.)

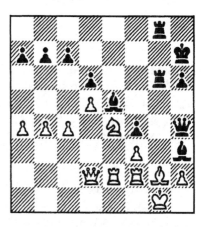

39. Black to play (15 mins.)

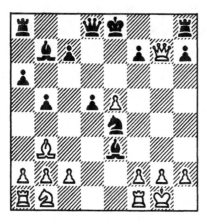

40. White to play (8 mins.)

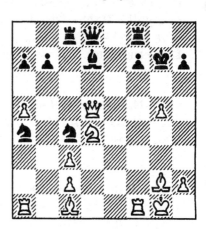

41. Black to play (7 mins.)

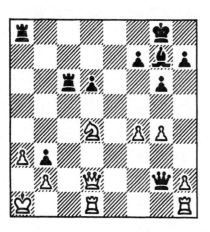

42. White to play (12 mins.)

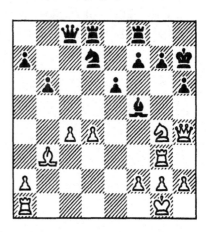

SOLUTIONS TO POSITIONS 37-42

37. Castanga-Feldman, Zurich, 1958

1 ♗d3!! ♕f6 (the bishop is taboo: *1... ♘xd3 2 ♕d7+ ♔f8 3 ♕d8* mate, or *1... ♕xd3 2 ♕f7+ ♔d8 3 e7+*) 2 e7! ♔f7 (or *2... ♕xe7 3 ♗g6+ ♔f8 4 ♕b8+*) 3 d6! ♗d5 (*3... ♘xd3 4 e8=♕+ ♔xe8 5 d7+*) 4 e8=♕+! ♔xe8 5 ♗g6+ Black resigns (*5... ♕xg6 6 ♕e7* mate, or *5... ♗f7 6 ♗xf7+ ♔f8 7 ♗d5*).

38. Tinworth-Farland, England, 1957

1... ♗d4! 2 ♕xd4 ♖xg2+ 3 ♖xg2 ♖xg2+ 4 ♔h1 (or *4 ♖xg2 ♕e1* mate) 4... ♖xe2 5 ♘f6+ ♕xf6 White resigns (*6 ♕xf6 ♖e1* mate).

39. Zaitsev-Rokhlin, Yaroslavl, 1954

1... ♕g5!! 2 ♕xh8+ ♔e7 3 ♕xh7 ♗xf2+! 4 ♔h1 (or *4 ♖xf2 ♕c1+ 5 ♖f1 ♕e3+ 6 ♔h1 ♘f2+*) 4... ♖g8 5 ♕h3 ♗c8! White resigns. 6 ♕f3 is met by 6... ♘g3+ 7 hxg3 ♕h6+ and mates.

40. Mista-Navarovszky, Reggio Emilia, 1967/68

1 ♖xa4! ♗xa4 2 ♖xf7+!! ♔h8 (on *2... ♖xf7* there follows *3 ♘e6+*) 3 ♖xh7+! ♔xh7 4 g6+ ♔xg6 5 ♗e4+! Black resigns.

41. Weller-Hall, Glasgow, 1964

1... ♖c1+!! 2 ♕xc1 ♖xa3+!! 3 ♔b1 (or 3 bxa3 ♕a2 mate) 3... ♖a1+!! 4 ♔xa1 ♕a8+ 5 ♔b1 ♕a2 mate.

42. Saprokhin-Arabkertsev, Volgograd, 1967

1 ♗c2! ♕xc4 (if *1... ♗xc2 2 ♘xh6 gxh6 3 ♖h3*) 2 ♘xh6! gxh6 3 ♖h3 f6 4 ♕xh6+ ♔g8 5 ♖g3+ ♔f7 6 ♖g7+ Black resigns.

43. Black to play (10 mins.)

44. White to play (12 mins.)

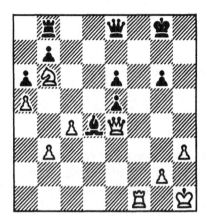

45. Black to play (15 mins.)

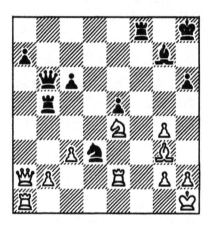

46. White to play (15 mins.)

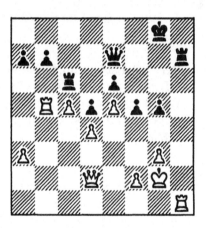

47. White to play (15 mins.)

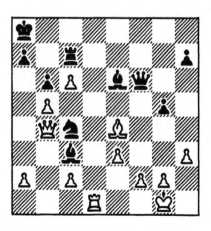

48. Black to play (8 mins.)

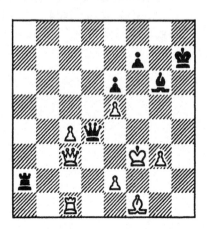

SOLUTIONS TO POSITIONS 43-48

43. Kogan-Sokolsky, Kiev, 1950

1...f5!! 2 ♗xf5 ♗xg3! 3 ♖fe1 ♗xf2+! 4 ♔xf2 ♛h2+ 5 ♔e3 ♖g3+ 6 ♔f3 ♖xf3+ 7 ♔xf3 ♖f8 8 ♔e4 ♛c2+ White resigns.

44. Podgayets-Zhuravlyov, Leningrad, 1974

1 ♘d7! ♛xd7 (in view of the threat of *2 ♘f6+*, Black is forced to accept this gift) 2 ♛xg6+ ♔g7 3 ♛xe6+ ♔h8 4 ♖f5! (after *4 ♖f7 ♛g5* Black could have resisted) 4...♖f8 5 ♖h5+ ♛h7 6 ♖xh7+ ♔xh7 7 ♛e7+ ♔g8 8 ♛xb7 Black resigns.

45. Pavlitzky-Rech, Halle, 1971

1...♖a5!! 2 ♛b1 ♖xa1 3 ♛xa1 ♛a6!! 4 ♛b1 *(4 ♛g1 ♘c5!* or *4 ♛d1 ♘xb2!)* 4...♘c1!! 5 ♛xc1 (or *5 ♖f2 ♛f1+!!*) 5...Qxe2 White resigns.

46. Byrne,R-Bachmann, Helsinki, 1952

1 ♖xb7!! ♛xb7 2 ♛xg5+ ♖g7 *(2...♔h8 3 ♛d8+ ♔g7 4 ♛f6+ ♔g8 5 ♛g6+ ♔h8 6 ♖xh7+ ♔xh7 7 ♛e8+, or 2...♛g7 3 ♛d8+ ♔f7 4 ♖xh7 ♛xh7 5 ♛d7+)* 3 ♛d8+ ♔f7 4 ♖h6! ♖g6 5 ♖h7+ ♖g7 6 ♛h8 Black resigns *(6...♔g6 7 ♖h6+ ♔f7 8 ♖f6+).*

47. Kreichik-N.N., Vienna, 1952

1 ♛xc3!! ♛f8 (or *1...♛xc3 2 ♖d8+ ♗c8 3 ♖xc8+ and 4 c7 mate*) 2 ♛g7!! ♛c8 3 ♛xc7!! ♛xc7 4 ♖d8+! ♛xd8 5 c7+ ♗d5 6 ♗xd5+ ♛xd5 7 c8=♛ mate.

48. Ivanov-Sveshnikov, Chelyabinsk, 1973

1...♖a3!! 2 ♛xa3 ♗e4+ 3 ♔f4 ♗g2+ 4 ♔g5 ♛xe5+ 5 ♔g4 ♛f5+ 6 ♔h4 ♛h3+ 7 ♔g5 ♛h6+ 8 ♔g4 f5 mate.

49. Black to play (10 mins.)

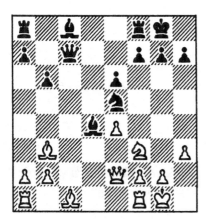

50. White to play (15 mins.)

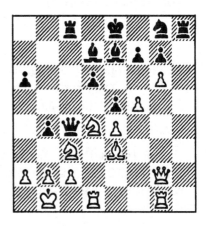

51. White to play (16 mins.)

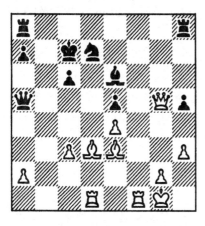

52. White to play (20 mins.)

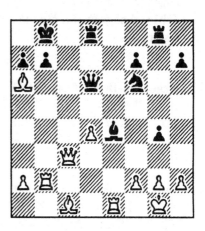

53. White to play (20 mins.)

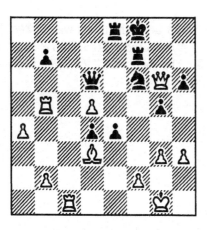

54. White to play (20 mins.)

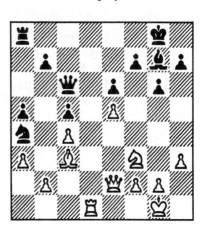

SOLUTIONS TO POSITIONS 49-54

49. Yasvoin-Kopayev, Leningrad, 1947
1...♗a6! 2 ♕xa6 ♘xf3+ 3 gxf3 ♕g3+ 4 ♔h1 ♕xf3+ 5 ♔g1 ♕g3+ 6 ♔h1 ♕xh3+ 7 ♔g1 ♗e5 White resigns.

50. Nezhmetdinov-Paoli, Bucharest, 1954
1 b3! ♕xc3 2 gxf7+ ♔d8 (or *2...♔xf7 3 ♕xg7+ ♔e8 4 ♕xh8*) 3 ♕xg7 exd4 4 ♗xd4 ♕xc2+ 5 ♔a1 ♖h2 6 ♗b6+ ♖c7 7 ♕xg8+ Black resigns.

51. Matsukevich-Alburt, Volgograd, 1968
1 ♗c4! ♗xc4 (or *1...♖ae8 2 ♗xe6 ♖xe6 3 ♖f7*) 2 ♖xd7+! ♔xd7 3 ♕g7+ ♔c8 (*3...♔e6 4 ♖f6 mate, or 3...♔d6 4 ♖d1+ ♗d5 5 exd5, and wins*) 4 ♕xh8+ ♔b7 5 ♖b1+ ♗b5 6 ♕g7+ ♔c7 (*6...♔a6 7 c4!!*) 7 ♕g6 ♔a6 8 ♕e6 ♖d8 9 ♕b3 Black resigns.

52. Negeieshi-Berta, Corr., 1971
1 ♗f4!! ♕xf4 2 ♗xb7 ♖d6 (if *2...♗xb7 3 ♖xb7+ ♔a8 4 ♕c6 ♕d6 5 ♖b8+ ♔xb8 6 ♖b1+*) 3 ♗c6+ ♔c8 4 ♗xe4+ ♔d8 5 ♖b8+ ♔d7 6 ♖b7+ ♔e8 7 ♕c8+ ♖d8 8 ♗d5+! ♘e4 9 ♗xf7+ Black resigns.

53. Buturin-Sergievsky, Lvov, 1972
1 ♖xb7! ♖xb7 2 ♖c6 ♖g7 3 ♕xh6 ♕xd5 (no better is *3...♕d8 4 ♖xf6+ ♔g8 5 ♗c4!*) 4 ♖xf6+ ♔g8 5 ♗b5 ♖f8 6 ♖c6 ♕d8 7 ♗c4+ ♖ff7 8 ♗xf7+ ♔xf7 9 ♕e6+ Black resigns.

54. Tal-Suttles, Sukhumi, 1972
1 ♗xa5! ♖xa5 2 ♖d8+ ♗f8 3 ♕d2 ♕c7 4 ♖e8 ♔g7 (the threat was *5 ♕h6 ♕e7 6 ♘g5!!*) 5 ♕g5 ♖a7 (no better is *5...♘b6 6 ♕f6+ ♔g8 7 ♘g5 ♖a8 8 ♘xe6 ♕c6 9 ♕g7 mate*) 6 ♕f6+ ♔g8 7 ♘g5 ♕d7 8 ♖d8 b6 (or *8...♕c7 9 ♖xf8+ ♔xf8 10 ♘xe6+*) 9 ♖xd7 ♖xd7 10 b3, and White won.

55. White to play (20 mins.)

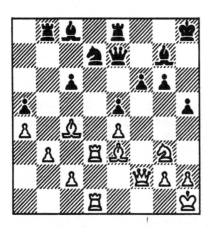

56. Black to play (20 mins.)

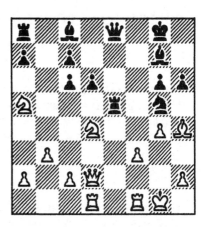

Theme: "Decoy" (Nos. 57-70)

57. White to play (8 mins.)

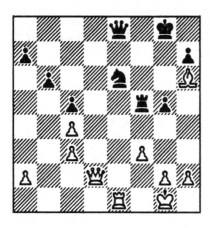

58. Black to play (10 mins.)

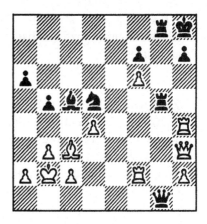

59. White to play (8 mins.)

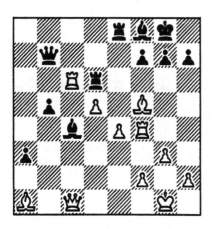

60. White to play (6 mins.)

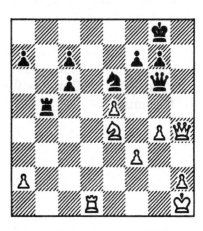

SOLUTIONS TO POSITIONS 55-60

55. Matulovic-Tringov, Siegen, 1970

1 Nf5!! gxf5 (Black cannot decline the sacrifice, since *1...Qf8*, for instance, fails to *2 Nh4! Kh7 3 Nxg6 Kxg6 4 Qf5 mate*) 2 Qh4 Nf8 3 Rxh5+ Nh7 4 Bc5!! Qxc5 5 Rh3 Bh6 6 Qxe8+ Qf8 7 Rd8! fxe4 8 Qxf8+ Bxf8 9 Rxf8+ Kg7 10 Rg8 mate.

56. Uitumen-Knesevic, Dubna, 1974

1...Rxa5! 2 Qxa5 Bxd4+ 3 Rxd4 Qe3+ 4 Bf2 Qxf3 (not *4...Nh3+ 5 Kg2 Nxf2 6 Qd2!*) 5 h4 Nh3+ 6 Kh2 Nxf2 7 Rd3 Nxg4+ 8 Kg1 Qe2 9 Qd2 Qxd2 10 Rxd2 h5 White resigns.

57. Furman-Boyarinov, Leningrad, 1965

1 Rxe6!! Qxe6 2 Qd8+ Qf7 3 Qf8+ Kg6 4 Qg7+ Kh5 5 g4+ Kh4 6 Bxg5+!! Black resigns (*6 gxf5 was bad on account of 6...Qe1+ 7 Kg2 Qe2+ 8 Kg1 Kh3, and mates*).

58. Zinn-Minev, Halle, 1967

1...Na3+!! 2 Kxa3 b4+ (*2...Qc1+ fails to win after 3 Bb2 b4+ 4 Ka4 Nb6+ 5 Kxb4 Rb5+ - or 5...Qe1+ 6 c3 - 6 Kc3, but not 6 Ka3? Nc4+*) 3 Ka4 (*3 Kb2 would have been answered by 3...bxc3+ 4 Ka3 Qc1+ 5 Ka4 Nb6+ 6 Kb4 a5+! 7 Kxc3 Rg3+!! 8 hxg3 Qe3+ 9 Kb2 Nc4+*) 3...Nb6+ 4 Kxb4 Rb5+ 5 Ka3 Qc1+ 6 Bb2 Nc4+! White resigns.

59. Sakharov-Cherepkov, Alma-Ata, 1969

1 Bxh7+!! Kxh7 2 Rxd6 Bxd6 3 Rh4+ Kg8 4 Rh8+!! Kxh8 5 Qh6+ Kg8 6 Qxg7 mate.

60. Kovacs-Beni, Vienna, 1950

1 Rd8+!! Nxd8 2 Qxd8+ Kh7 3 Ng5+ Kh6 4 Nxf7+! Rxf7 5 Qh4+ Kg6 6 Qh5 mate.

61. White to play (12 mins.)

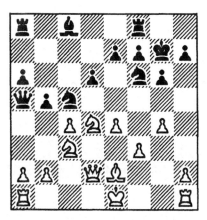

62. White to play (10 mins.)

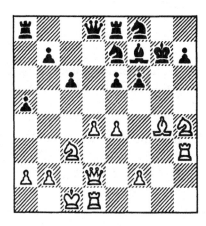

63. Black to play (12 mins.)

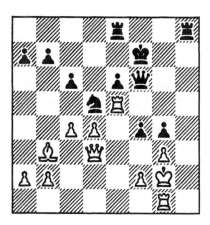

64. Black to play (15 mins.)

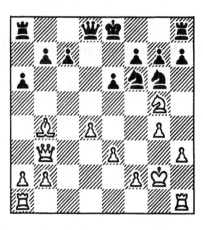

65. White to play (15 mins.)

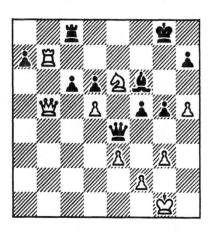

66. White to play (12 mins.)

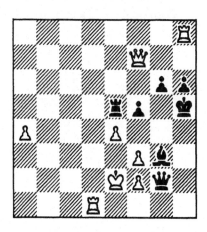

SOLUTIONS TO POSITIONS 61-66

61. Hernandez-Rantanen, Skopje, 1972

1 g5! ♘h5 2 b4!! ♕xb4 3 ♘c6 ♕a3 4 ♘b1 ♕a4 5 ♕b2+ e5 6 ♘c3! Black resigns.

62. Hansuit-Brunner, Porto Rico, 1965

1 ♕h6+!! ♔xh6 (or *1...♔g8 2 ♗xe6! ♘xe6 3 ♖g1+ ♘g6 4 ♘xg6 ♗xg6 5 ♕xh7+*) 2 ♘f5+ ♔g5 3 ♖g1! ♕xd4 (or *3...exf5 4 ♗xf5+*) 4 ♗e2+ ♔f4 5 ♖h4+ ♔e5 6 f4 mate.

63. Grundinin-Rozit, Corr., 1959

1...♘e3+! 2 fxe3 ♖h2+!! 3 ♔xh2 fxg3+ 4 ♔xg3 (if *4 ♖xg3 ♕f2+!*) 4...♕f3+ 5 ♔h4 ♕h3+ 6 ♔g5 ♖g8+ 7 ♔f4 ♕f3 mate.

64. Vladimirov-Vorotnikov, Leningrad, 1973

1...♘h4+ 2 ♔g3 (*2 ♔f1 is bad on account of 2...♕d7!, threatening 3...♕b5+ and 4...♕xg5, as well as 3...♕c6 and 3...h6*; White cannot meet all these threats) 2...♘h5+!! 3 ♔xh4 h6! 4 f4 hxg5+ 5 fxg5 ♕xg5+!! 6 ♔xg5 f6+ 7 ♔g6 (or *7 ♔h4 g5 mate*) 7...♖h6 mate.

65. Nersisyan-Krementsky, Moscow, 1968

1 ♖g7+!! ♗xg7 2 ♕b7!! ♗h6 3 ♕xc8+ ♔f7 4 ♕d7+ ♔f6 5 ♕xh7 ♔e5 6 ♘c7 ♕b1+ 7 ♔g2 ♔e4 8 g4 Black resigns.

66. Bena-Ksarko, Rumania, 1971

1 ♖xh6+! ♔xh6 2 ♕f8+ ♔g5 3 ♕d8+ ♔h5 4 ♖h1+! ♕xh1 5 ♕h8+ ♔g5 6 ♕xh1 ♗f4 7 ♕g1+ ♔f6 8 ♕a1 Black resigns.

67. White to play (15 mins.)

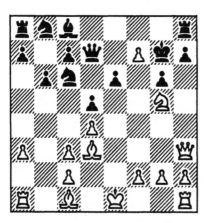

68. White to play (12 mins.)

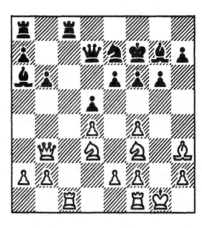

69. White to play (20 mins.)

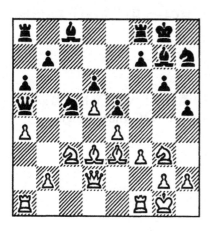

70. White to play (15 mins.)

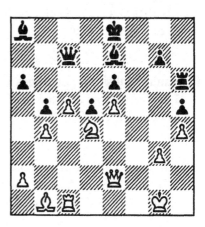

Theme: "Interference" (Nos. 71-74)

71. White to play (12 mins.)

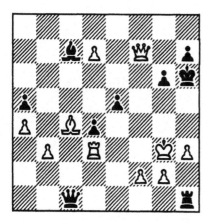

72. White to play (15 mins.)

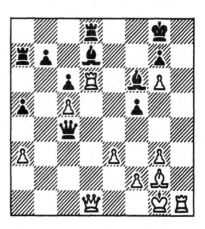

SOLUTIONS TO POSITIONS 67-72

67. **Scheinke-Bogkof, Corr., 1963**
    1 ♕h6+!! ♔xh6 2 ♘xe6+ g5 (if *2...♔h5 3 ♗e2+ ♔h4 4 ♗g5* mate) 3 ♗xg5+
    ♔h5 4 g4+! ♔xg4 5 ♖g1+ ♔h3 6 ♘f4+ ♔xh2 7 ♖g2+ ♔h1 8 ♘d2 mate.

68. **Utkin-Amosov, Moscow, 1951**
    1 ♘de5+! fxe5 2 ♗xe6+! ♔xe6 3 ♘g5+ ♔d6 (if *3...♔f6 4 dxe5+ ♔f5 5 ♕h3+*) 4
    ♕a3+ ♖c5 5 dxc5+ ♔c7 6 cxb6+ ♔d8 7 ♕xa6, and White won.

69. **Korchnoi-Balashov, Moscow, 1971**
    1 b4!! ♕xb4 2 a5! ♗h6 3 ♗xh6 ♘b3 4 ♕b2 ♕d4+ 5 ♖f2 ♘xa1 6 ♗xf8 h4 7
    ♘ge2! Black resigns.

70. **Tanin-Maksimov, Leningrad, 1951**
    1 ♗g6+!! ♖xg6 2 ♕xh5 ♔f7 3 ♖f1+ ♗f6 4 ♖xf6+! gxf6 5 ♕h7+ ♖g7 6 ♕xg7+
    ♔xg7 7 ♘xe6+ ♔f7 8 ♘xc7 ♗b7 9 exf6 ♔xf6 10 ♔f2 Black resigns.

71. **Bakhtiar-Mukhitdinov, Tashkent, 1959**
    1 ♖e3!! ♕a3 (on *1...dxe3* there follows *2 ♕f8+ ♔h5 3 ♗e2+ ♔g5 4 d8=♕+
    ♗xd8 5 f4+!!*) 2 ♖e4 ♗d8 3 ♖xe5! ♕d6 4 ♕f4+! g5 5 ♖e6+ ♕xe6 6 ♕f8+
    Black resigns.

72. **Kevorkov-Tarasov, Omsk, 1950**
    1 ♗d5+!! cxd5 2 ♖h8+!! ♔xh8 3 ♕h5+ ♔g8 4 ♕h7+ ♔f8 5 ♖xf6+! ♔e8 6
    ♕g8+ ♔e7 7 ♕f7 mate.

73. Black to play (12 mins.)

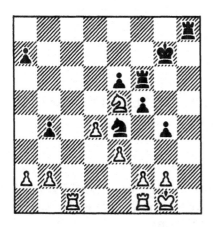

74. White to play (25 mins.)

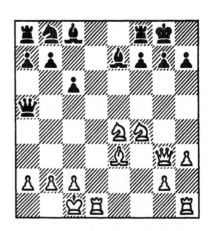

Theme: "Defence-elimination" (Nos.75-86)

75. White to play (6 mins.)

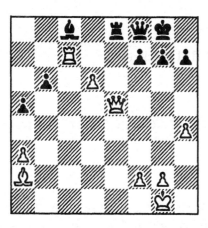

76. White to play (8 mins.)

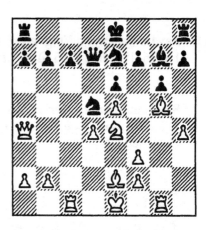

77. White to play (8 mins.)

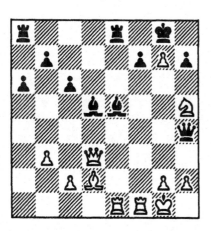

78. White to play (8 mins.)

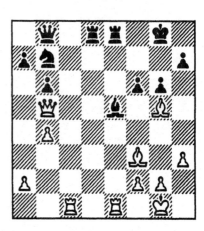

SOLUTIONS TO POSITIONS 73-78

73. Kroitsaller-Laipold, Tsitau, 1973

1... ♘c3!! 2 f4 (or *2 bxc3 ♖fh6 3 f3 g3!*) 2...g3! 3 ♖xc3 bxc3 4 ♖f3 cxb2 5 ♖xg3+ ♔f8 6 ♘d7+ ♔e7 7 ♖g7+ ♖f7 White resigns.

74. Mabbs-Alexander, London, 1961

1 ♖d5!! cxd5 2 ♘h5 g6 3 ♘hf6+ ♗xf6 4 ♘xf6+ ♔g7 (or *4...♔h8 5 ♕h4!*) 5 ♕e5! ♔h8 6 ♗h6 ♘c6 7 ♗g7+!! ♔xg7 8 ♘e8+ ♔h6 9 ♕f4+ g5 (or *9...♔h5 10 ♘g7* mate) 10 ♕f6+ ♔h5 11 ♘g7+ ♔h4 12 ♕f2 mate.

75. Filip-Ubranek, Prague, 1955

1 ♕xe8!! ♕xe8 2 ♗xf7+!! ♕xf7 3 ♖xc8+ ♕f8 4 d7! Black resigns.

76. Zayats-Taskayev, Volgograd, 1956

1 ♘d6+!! cxd6 2 ♗b5 ♘c6 3 ♖xc6! 0-0 4 ♖c1 Black resigns.

77. Szmetan-Juarez, Buenos Aires, 1972

1 ♖xe5!! ♖xe5 2 ♘f6+ ♔xg7 3 ♗c3 ♕xf6 4 ♖xf6 ♔xf6 5 ♕d4 Black resigns (*5... ♖ae8 6 ♕f4+*).

78. Polugayevsky-Bilek, Busum, 1969

1 ♖xe5!! ♖xe5 (or *1...fxe5 2 ♕c4+ ♔g7 3 ♕c7+*) 2 ♕c4+ ♔g7 3 ♕c7+ ♔g8 4 ♗xf6 ♖e1+ 5 ♔h2 Black resigns (*5... ♖xc1* is met by *6 ♗d5+! ♔f8 7 ♗g7+ ♔e8 8 ♗f7* mate).

79. White to play (8 mins.)

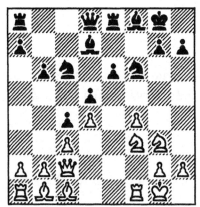

80. White to play (6 mins.)

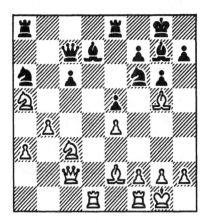

81. Black to play (6 mins.)

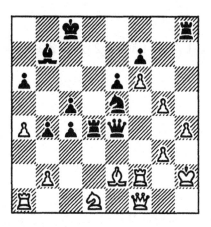

82. Black to play (8 mins.)

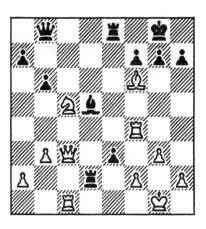

83. Black to play (15 mins.)

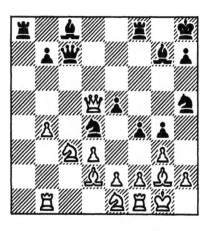

84. White to play (15 mins.)

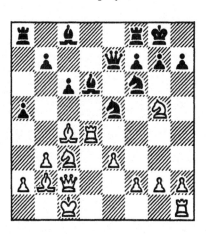

SOLUTIONS TO POSITIONS 79-84

79. Tukmakov-Guss, Graz, 1972
1 ♘g5 h6 (or *1...g6 2 ♘xh7!*) 2 ♘h5! ♗d6 (mate by *3 ♘xf6+* and *4 ♕h7* was threatened) 3 ♘f7!! ♕e7 (*3...♗xf7 4 ♕g6+* and *5 ♕xg7* mate) 4 ♘xd6 ♕xd6 5 ♘xf6+ Black resigns.

80. Hohler-Czerniak, Heidenheim, 1959
1 ♗xa6 ♖xa6 2 ♗xf6 ♗xf6 3 ♘d5! ♕d8 4 ♘xf6+ ♕xf6 5 ♖xd7 Black resigns.

81. Nilsson-Ciaceli, Stockholm, 1965
1...♖xd1!! 2 ♖xd1 ♖xh4+!! 3 gxh4 ♕xh4+ 4 ♕h3 ♕xf2+ 5 ♕g2 ♕xg2 mate.

82. Ferholt-Enklaar, Amsterdam, 1971
1...♕xf4!! 2 gxf4 exf2+ 3 ♔f1 ♖e1+! 4 ♖xe1 ♗g2+! 5 ♔xg2 fxe1=♕+ White resigns.

83. Lewi-Adamski, Polanica Zdroj, 1969
1...♕xc3!! 2 ♗xc3 ♘xe2+ 3 ♔h1 ♘xc3 4 ♕b3 ♘xb1 5 ♕xb1 f3 6 ♗xf3 gxf3 7 ♖g1 ♗h3 White resigns.

84. Petri-Both, West Germany, 1966
1 ♖xd6!! ♕xd6 2 ♘ce4 ♘xe4 3 ♕xe4 ♘g6 4 ♘xf7! ♖xf7 (if *4...♕e7 5 ♘e5+!*) 5 ♕e8+ ♕f8 6 ♗xf7+ ♔h8 7 ♗xg6 Black resigns.

85. Black to play (15 mins.)

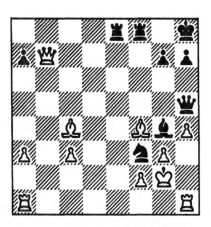

86. Black to play (20 mins.)

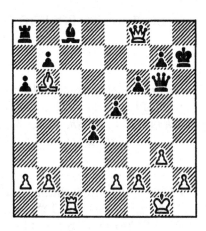

Theme: "Square-vacation" (Nos. 87-94)

87. White to play (7 mins.)

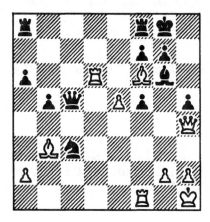

88. Black to play (12 mins.)

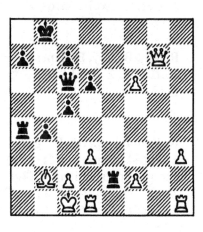

89. White to play (10 mins.)

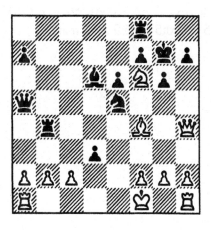

90. White to play (15 mins.)

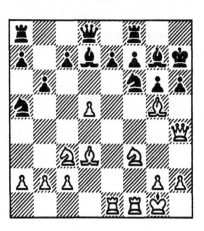

SOLUTIONS TO POSITIONS 85-90

85. Barcza-Keller, Moscow, 1956

1... ♖xf4!! 2 gxf4 ♗f5! 3 ♕xf3 (on *3 ♕d5* Black had prepared *3... ♕g4+ 4 ♔f1 ♕h3+ 5 ♖xh3 ♗xh3 mate*) 3...♗e4 4 ♖h3 ♕g4+ 5 ♖g3 ♕xf4 6 ♘d5 (if *6 ♖e1 ♗xf3+ 7 ♖xf3 ♕xf3+ 8 ♔xf3 ♖xe1*) 6...♗xf3+ 7 ♘xf3 ♕xh4 White resigns.

86. Kitanov-Baum, Sterlitamak, 1949

1...♘h3!! 2 ♕a3! (on *2 ♕xa8* there follows *2... ♕e4! 3 f3 ♕e3+*) 2...♖c8! 3 ♖e1 (*3 ♖xc8? ♕b1+*) 3...♖c3!! 4 bxc3 ♕e4 5 f3 ♕e3+ 6 ♔h1 ♕f2 7 ♖g1 ♕xe2 8 cxd4 e4! 9 f4 e3! White resigns.

87. Kottnauer-Lokvenc, Vienna, 1949

1 ♗xg7!! ♔xg7 2 ♕f6+ ♔h7 3 ♗xf7! ♗xf7 4 ♕h6+ ♔g8 5 ♕g5+ Black resigns.

88. Redely-Baraty, Budapest, 1961

1...♖a1+!! 2 ♗xa1 ♕a4! 3 ♕g8+ ♔b7 4 ♕b3 ♕xa1+ 5 ♔b1 ♖xc2+! 6 ♔xc2 ♕c3 mate.

89. Kubanek-Kopriva, Prague, 1952

1 ♕h6+! (if instead *1 ♕xh7+? ♔xf6 2 ♕h4+ ♔g7! 3 ♗h6+ ♔h7!*, and there is no decisive continuation) 1...♔xf6 2 ♕h4+! ♔f5 (*2... ♔g7* fails to *3 ♗h6+ ♔g8 4 ♕f6*) 3 ♕g5+ ♔e4 4 ♖e1+ ♔d5 (or 4...♔d4 5 ♗xe5+ ♗xe5 6 c3+ ♔c4 7 ♖e4+) 5 ♖xe5+ ♗xe5 6 ♕xe5+ Black resigns.

90. Diemer-Kotek, Corr., 1955

1 d6! cxd6 2 ♖xe7!! ♕xe7 3 ♘d5 ♕e6 4 ♘xf6+ ♗xf6 5 ♗xf6 ♕e3+ 6 ♔h1 Black resigns. On 6...♔g8 comes 7 ♘g5 h5 8 ♕xh5 gxh5 9 ♗h7 mate.

91. White to play (15 mins.)

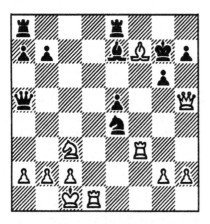

92. Black to play (18 mins.)

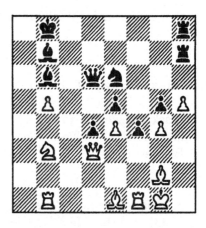

93. White to play (20 mins.)

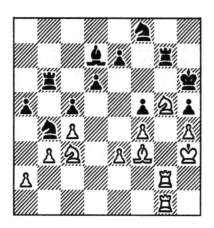

94. White to play (20 mins.)

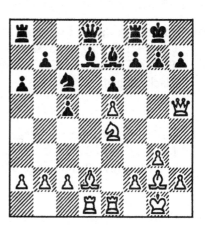

Theme: "Line-opening" (Nos. 95-122)

95. Black to play (10 mins.)

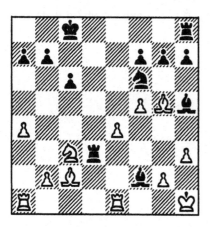

96. White to play (10 mins.)

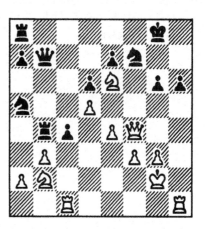

SOLUTIONS TO POSITIONS 91-96

91. Lipsky-Penczak, Lublin, 1964
1 ♗xg6!! hxg6 2 ♖f7+!! ♔xf7 3 ♕h7+ ♔e6 (in the event of *3...♔f8 4 ♘xe4*
Black, despite his extra rook, is unable to avoid defeat, e.g. *4...♕a6 5 ♖d3!*, with the
threat of *♖f3+*) 4 ♕xg6+ ♘f6 5 ♘e4 ♕d5 6 ♖xd5 ♔xd5 7 ♘xf6+ ♗xf6 8 ♕xf6
Black resigns.

92. Akopian-Ovsepian, Yerevan, 1972
1...f3!! 2 ♗xf3 ♘f4 3 ♕d2 d3+ 4 ♔h2 ♗xe4! 5 ♗xe4 ♖xh5+ 6 gxh5 ♖xh5+ 7
♔g3 ♕e6 White resigns.

93. Smyslov-Magrin, Lugano, 1968
1 ♘f7+!! ♖xf7 2 ♖g5 ♘g6 3 ♖xg6+ ♔h7 4 ♖6g5 d5 (*4...♔h8 5 ♗xh5*, or
4... ♖f6 5 a3 and *6 ♘d5*) 5 ♘xd5 ♘xd5 6 ♗xd5 ♖f8 7 ♖xh5+ ♖h6 8 ♗g8+!
Black resigns.

94. Reshevsky-Matumoto, Siegen, 1970
1 ♘f6+!! gxf6 2 exf6 ♗xf6 3 ♗e4! ♖e8 4 ♕xh7+ ♔f8 5 ♗g6!! ♗g7 6 ♗h6! ♕f6
7 ♖xd7 ♘e7 8 ♕h8+ ♘g8 9 ♕xg7+! Black resigns.

95. Grozdev-Meistr, Corr., 1954
1... ♖xh3+!! 2 gxh3 ♗f3+ 3 ♔h2 ♘g4+!! 4 hxg4 h5!! 5 ♗h6 hxg4! White resigns
(but not *5... ♖xh6 6 g5!*).

96. Filip-Uhlmann, Marianske Lazne/Prague, 1954
1 ♖xh6!! ♘xh6 2 ♖h1! ♖xb3 (or *2... ♘f7 3 ♖h7!*) 3 axb3 ♕xb3 4 ♘d1 ♘f7 5
♖h7! Black resigns.

97. Black to play (5 mins.)

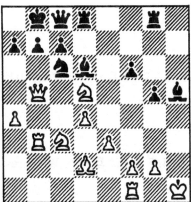

98. Black to play (10 mins.)

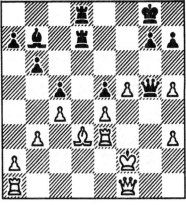

99. White to play (12 mins).

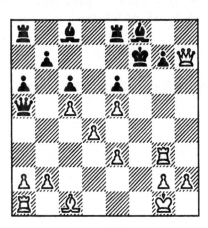

100. White to play (8 mins.)

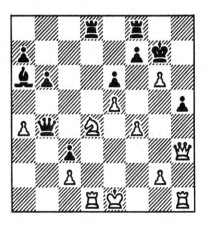

101. White to play (6 mins.)

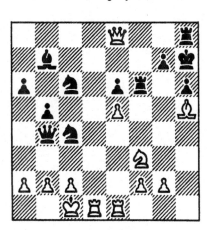

102. White to play (12 mins.)

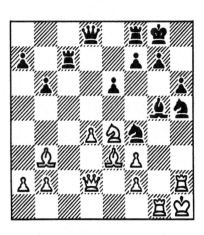

SOLUTIONS TO POSITIONS 97-102

97. Manov-Hairabedian, Bulgaria, 1962
1...♗e2!! 2 ♘xe2 (*2 ♕xe2* is no better) 2...♖h8+ 3 ♔g1 ♖h1+! 4 ♔xh1 ♖h8+ 5 ♔g1 ♖h1+! 6 ♔xh1 ♕h8+ 7 ♔g1 ♕h2 mate.

98. Cardoso-Ivkov, Marlborough, 1974
1...♗xe4!! 2 ♗xe4 ♕f4+ 3 ♗f3 ♖d2+ 4 ♖e2 e4! 5 ♖xd2 ♖xd2+ White resigns.

99. Benesch-Mich, Marianske Lazne, 1952
1 ♗d2!! ♕xd2 (other queen moves would be met in the same way) 2 ♖xg7+!! (after *2 ♖f1+ ♔e7 3 ♕h4+ ♔d7* the outcome would still be unclear) 2...♗xg7 3 ♖f1+ ♔e7 4 ♕h4+! ♗f6 (or *4...♔d7 5 ♖f7+* and *6 ♕xe7* mate) 5 exf6+ Black resigns. On 5...♔d7 there follows 6 ♕g3 e5 7 f7 ♖f8 8 ♕xe5 and 9 ♕d6+.

100. Nei-Zeinaly, Tallinn, 1948
1 ♕xh5 ♖h8 2 ♘xe6+!! fxe6 3 ♖d7+! ♖xd7 4 ♕xh8+ ♔xg6 5 ♕f6 mate.

101. Golan-Stiv, Budapest, 1950
1 ♘g5+!! hxg5 2 ♗g6+! ♖xg6 3 ♖h1+ ♖h6 4 ♖xh6+ gxh6 (or *4...♔xh6 5 ♖h1* mate) 5 ♕f7 mate.

102. Lutsenko-Vardanian, Moscow, 1952
1 ♖xh5!! ♘xh5 2 ♗xg5 hxg5 3 ♖xg5 g6 (if *3...♘f6 4 ♖xg7+! ♔xg7 5 ♕g5+ ♔h8 6 ♘xf6*) 4 ♖xh5! gxh5 5 ♕h6 ♕xd4 6 ♘f6+ Black resigns.

103. White to play (10 mins.)

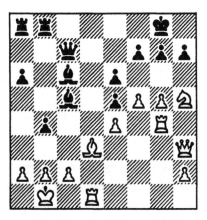

104. White to play (12 mins.)

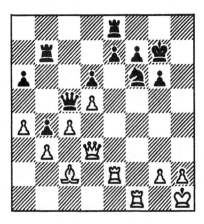

105. Black to play (10 mins.)

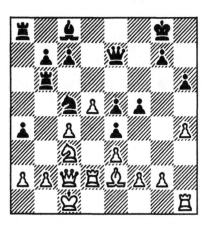

106. White to play (6 mins.)

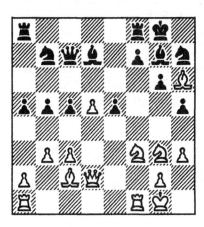

107. White to play (6 mins.)

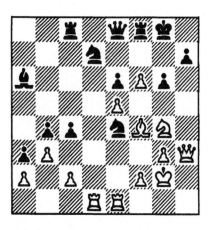

108. White to play (10 mins.)

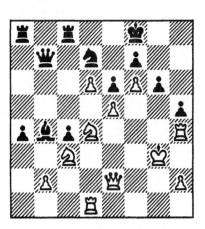

SOLUTIONS TO POSITIONS 103-108

103. Madoni-Minaja, Tel Aviv, 1964
1 ♘f6+!! gxf6 (or *1...♔f8 2 ♕xh7!*) 2 gxf6+ ♔f8 3 ♖g8+!! ♔xg8 4 ♕h6! ♗f8 5 ♖g1+ ♔h8 6 ♖g7! Black resigns.

104. Chukayev-Malev, Kaunas, 1964
1 ♖xf6!! ♔xf6 2 ♖e6+! ♔g7 (if *2...fxe6 3 ♕xg6+ ♔e5 4 ♕g7+ ♔f4 5 ♕g3* mate) 3 ♖xg6+! fxg6 (or *3...♔f8 4 ♖g8+!*) 4 ♕xg6+ ♔f8 5 ♕h6+ ♔f7 6 ♗g6+ ♔f6 7 ♗h7+ Black resigns.

105. Movshovich-Tribushevsky, Moscow, 1956
1...♘b3+! 2 axb3 axb3 3 ♕d1 (or *3 ♕b1 ♖ba6!*) 3...♖a1+ 4 ♘b1 ♕b4 5 d6 ♕a4 6 d7 ♖xb1+ White resigns.

106. Smejkal-Medina, Amsterdam, 1971
1 ♘xh5!! gxh5 2 ♗xh7+ ♔xh7 3 ♗xg7 ♔xg7 4 ♕g5+ ♔h7 5 ♕xh5+ ♔g7 6 ♘g5! Black resigns.

107. Platz-Just, Leipzig, 1972
1 ♕xh7+!! ♔xh7 2 ♖h1+ ♔g8 3 ♘h6+ ♔h7 4 ♘f7+ ♔g8 5 ♖h8+!! ♔xf7 6 ♖h7+ Black resigns (*6...♔g8 7 ♖g7+ ♔h8 8 ♖h1* mate).

108. Sanakoyev-Zagorovsky, Voronezh, 1972
1 ♖xh5!! gxh5 2 ♕xh5 ♘e8 3 ♘xe6!! ♘f8 4 d7+! ♘xd7 5 ♕h8+ ♗f8 6 ♕xf8+!! ♘xf8 7 ♘g7 mate. In the game White played the weaker 6 ♘g7+ ♔d8 7 ♕xf8+, and won, but only after a prolonged struggle.

109. White to play (12 mins.)

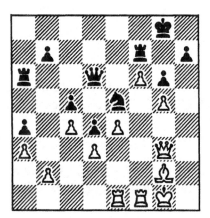

110. White to play (15 mins.)

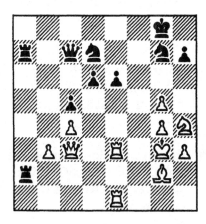

111. Black to play (15 mins.)

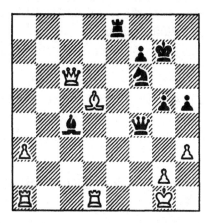

112. White to play (18 mins.)

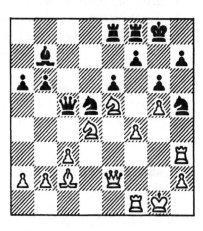

113. Black to play (20 mins.)

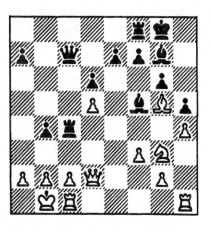

114. Black to play (18 mins.)

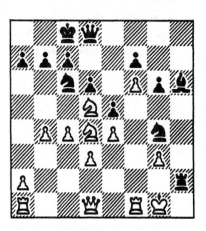

SOLUTIONS TO POSITIONS 109-114

109. Johannsson-N.N., Reykjavik, 1960
1 ♖f5!! gxf5 (if *1... ♘xc4 2 e5 ♕e6 3 dxc4 ♕xf5 4 ♗h3! and 5 e6!*) 2 exf5 ♘xc4 3 ♖e8+ ♖f8 4 ♗d5+! ♕xd5 5 ♖xf8+ ♔xf8 6 ♕b8+ ♔f7 7 ♕c7+ Black resigns.

110. Rossetto-Cardoso, Portoroz, 1958
1 ♗d5!! exd5 2 ♕xg7+!! ♔xg7 3 ♘f5+ ♔g6 (or *3... ♔g8 4 ♘h6+!, but not 4 ♖e8+ ♘f8*) 4 ♖e6+ ♗f6 5 ♖xf6+ ♔xg5 6 ♖ee6 ♖g2+ 7 ♔xg2 ♕d8 8 ♘e7! Black resigns.

111. Kasas-Debarnot, Buenos Aires, 1972
With his last move White had captured a pawn with 1 ♗f3xd5. There followed:
1...♘g4! 2 hxg4 (forced, otherwise White is mated) 2...♕e3+ 3 ♔h2 ♖h8!! 4 ♗f3 hxg4+ 5 ♔g3 ♕f4+ 6 ♔f2 g3+ 7 ♔g1 ♖h1+!! White resigns.

112. Benau-Jiffar, Messeri, 1974
1 ♖xh5! gxh5 2 ♗xh7+! ♔xh7 3 ♕xh5+ ♔g8 4 g6 ♔g7 5 gxf7 ♘e7 6 fxe8=♘+ ♔g8 7 ♕g5+ ♔h8 8 ♕g7 mate.

113. Grabenweger-Herzog, Vienna, 1973
1...♗c3!! 2 ♕e2 b3! 3 axb3 (no better is *3 ♘xf5 bxa2+ 4 ♔a1 ♖b4!*) 3...♖a4! 4 ♘xf5 (or *4 bxc3 ♕xc3 5 bxa4 ♕b3+ 6 ♔a1 ♕xa4+*) 4...♖a5 5 ♘xe7+ ♔h7 6 bxa4 ♖b8 7 ♖cf1 ♖xb2+ 8 ♔c1 ♖b1+! White resigns.

114. Demeny-Beszterczei, Debrecen, 1957
1...♗e3+! 2 ♘xe3 ♖h1+! 3 ♔g2 (or *3 ♔xh1 ♕h8+ 4 ♔g2 ♕h2+ 5 ♔f3 ♘xd4+ 6 ♔xg4 ♕h5 mate*) 3...♘xe3+ 4 ♔xh1 ♘xd1 5 ♘xc6 ♕h8+ 6 ♔g1 ♘e3 7 ♘e7+ ♔d7 8 ♖f3 ♘g4 White resigns.

115. Black to play (16 mins.)

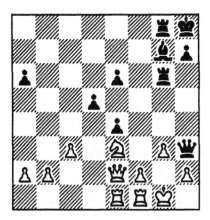

116. Black to play (18 mins.)

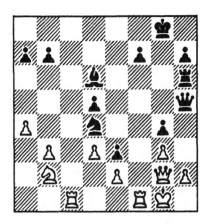

117. White to play (15 mins.)

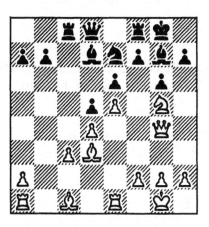

118. Black to play (15 mins.)

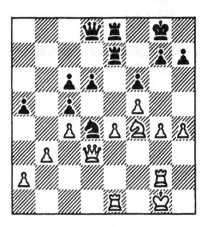

119. Black to play (20 mins.)

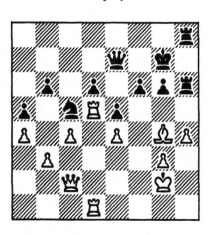

120. White to play (20 mins.)

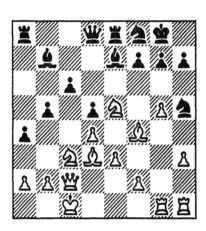

SOLUTIONS TO POSITIONS 115-120

115. Balinas-Korchnoi, Lugano, 1968
1...♗xc3!! 2 bxc3 ♖h6 3 f3 ♖xg3+! 4 ♘h1 exf3 5 ♕b2 ♖g2 6 ♕b8+ ♔g7 7 ♘f5+ ♕xf5 8 ♖g1 ♕h3 9 ♕e5+ ♔f7 10 ♕f4+ ♔g6 White resigns.

116. Nebilitsin-Karpenko, Novosibirsk, 1971
1...♗xg3!! 2 ♖c8+ (or *2 hxg3 ♘xe2+! 3 ♕xe2 ♕h1 mate*, while Black was threatening *2...♗xh2+ 3 ♘h1 ♗g3+ 4 ♔g1 ♘xe2+! 5 ♕xe2 ♕h1 mate*) 2...♔g7 3 h4 ♘xe2+! (not *3...♕xh4? 4 ♖xf7+ ♔xf7 5 ♕xd5+*) 4 ♕xe2 ♕xh4 5 ♕g2 ♗h2+ 6 ♔h1 ♗f4+ 7 ♔g1 e2 8 ♖e8 ♗h2+ 9 ♔h1 exf1=♕+ 10 ♕xf1 ♗g1+ White resigns.

117. Barendregt-Szilagyi, Amsterdam, 1966
1 ♘xh7! ♔xh7 2 ♕h4+ ♔g8 3 ♗g5 ♖e8 4 ♖e3 ♖xc3 5 ♖h3 ♖xd3 6 ♕h7+ ♔f8 7 ♗f6!! ♘f5 8 ♕h8+ Black resigns.

118. Krikunov-Chernenko, Rostov, 1974
1...d5! 2 cxd5 (forced, otherwise *2...dxe4*, with a quick win) 2...cxd5 3 ♘xd5 ♕xd5!! 4 exd5 ♖xe1+ 5 ♔h2 ♖8e3! 6 ♕a6 ♘f3+ 7 ♔g3 ♗g5+ 8 ♔f2 ♘h3 mate.

119. Ivkov-Quinteros, Olot, 1974
1...f5! 2 exf5 ♖xh4!! 3 gxh4 ♕xh4 4 f6+ ♔f7 5 ♔f3 e4+ 6 ♔f4 ♘e6+ (stronger than *6...g5+*) 7 ♔e3 ♕g3+ 8 ♔d2 ♖h2+ 9 ♗e2 ♖xe2+!! White resigns.

120. Averbakh-Sarvarov, Moscow, 1959
1 ♗xh7+! ♘xh7 2 g6! fxg6 3 ♕xg6 ♘7f6 4 ♕f7+ ♔h8 (if *4...♔h7 5 ♖g6!*) 5 ♖xg7! ♘xg7 6 ♖g1 ♘fh5 7 ♖g6! ♕d6 8 ♖xd6 ♗xd6 9 ♘g6+ Black resigns.

121. White to play (20 mins.)

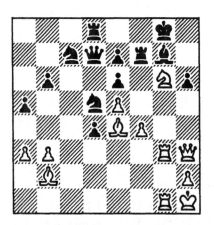

122. White to play (18 mins.)

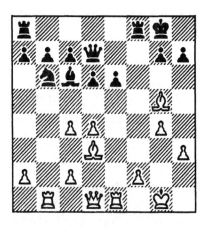

Theme: "Utilization of open files" (Nos. 123-130)

123. Black to play (5 mins.)

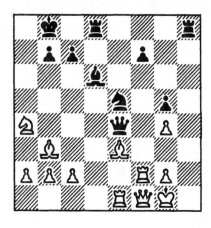

124. White to play (7 mins.)

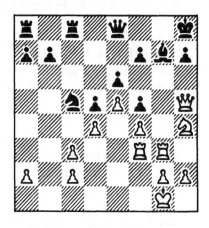

125. Black to play (12 mins.)

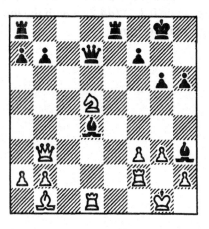

126. White to play (10 mins.)

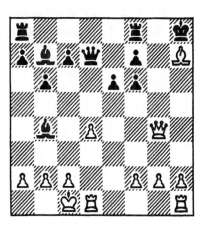

SOLUTIONS TO POSITIONS 121-126

121. Turukin-Mitin, Corr., 1974
1 ♘f8!! ♔xf8 2 ♕xh6! ♔e8 (the threat was *3 ♕h8+ and 4 ♖g8 mate*) 3 ♕h8+
♗f8 4 ♕xf8+! ♖xf8 5 ♗g6+ ♖f7 6 ♗xf7+ ♔xf7 7 ♖g7+ ♔e8 8 ♖g8+ ♔f7 9
♖1g7 mate.

122. Hartston-Bouwmeester, Adelboden, 1969
1 d5! exd5 2 ♖e7 ♕c8 3 ♗xh7+ ♔xh7 (or *3...♔h8 4 ♕d4!*) 4 ♕d3+ ♖f5 (if
4...♔h8 5 ♕g6 ♖g8 6 ♕h5 mate) 5 gxf5 dxc4 6 ♕d4 ♕f8 7 ♕h4+ ♔g8 8 f6!
Black resigns.

123. Suni-Alivitra, Helsinki, 1957
1...♖h1+!! 2 ♔xh1 ♕h7+ 3 ♔g1 ♕h2+!! 4 ♔xh2 ♘f3+ 5 ♔h3 ♖h8 mate.

124. Herzog-Banas, Milan, 1974
1 ♖xg7! ♔xg7 2 ♘xf5+!! ♔h8 (if *2...exf5 3 ♕g5+ ♔f8 4 ♕h6+*) 3 ♕g5 exf5 4
♕f6+ ♔g8 5 ♖g3+ ♔f8 6 ♕h6+ Black resigns (*6...♔e7 7 ♕d6 mate*).

125. Nielsen-Oren, Amsterdam, 1954
1...♖e2!! 2 ♘f6+ ♔h8 3 ♘xd7 ♗xf2+ (*3...♖xf2 fails to win after 4 ♔h1 ♗g2+ 5
♔g1*) 4 ♔h1 ♗d4! 5 ♖g1 ♗g2+ 6 ♖xg2 ♖e1+ 7 ♖g1 ♖xg1 mate.

126. Jansa-Marovic, Madonna di Campiglio, 1974
1 d5!! (if *1 ♖d3 ♕d5*, when *2 ♖h3* is met by *2...♕g5+*, and *2 ♗f5* by *2...♕xf5 3
♖h3+ ♕h7*) 1...♖fd8 (on *1...f5* there follows *2 ♗xf5 exf5 3 ♕h5+ ♔g7 4 ♕g5+
♔h7 5 ♖d3 f4 6 ♖g3!* with inevitable mate, while if *1...♕a4 2 c3* with the threat of
3 ♗c2) 2 ♖d3! ♗xd5 3 ♗f5 ♗xg2 4 ♕xg2 Black resigns.

127. Black to play (12 mins.)   **128.** White to play (15 mins.)

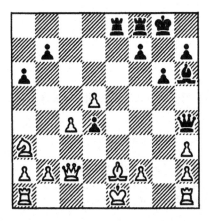   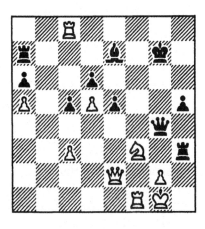

129. White to play (20 mins.)   **130.** Black to play (20 mins.)

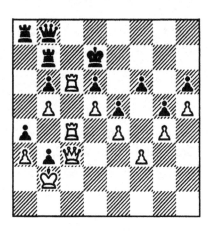   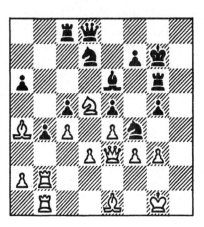

Theme: "Diagonal-opening" (Nos. 131-150)

131. Black to play (5 mins.)   **132.** Black to play (7 mins.)

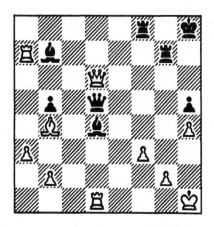   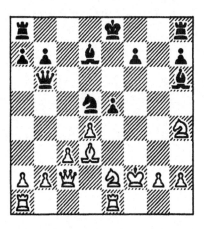

SOLUTIONS TO POSITIONS 127-132

127. Zhelyandinov-Shakhov, Perm, 1960
1...d3!! 2 ♕xd3 ♖e3! 3 ♕d1 ♖fe8 4 0-0 ♖xe2 5 ♕b3 ♗e3 6 ♘c2 ♗xf2+ White resigns.

128. Karpov-Zsoldos, Budapest, 1973 (from a simultaneous display)
1 ♘xe5!! ♕xe2 2 ♖f7+ ♔h6 3 ♖h8+ ♔g5 4 ♖g8+ ♔h4 (or *4...♔h6 5 ♖g6* mate) 5 ♘g6+ ♔g5 (if *5...♔g3 6 ♘xe7+ ♔g4 7 ♖xg4+*, and wins) 6 ♘xe7+ ♔h4 7 ♘f5 mate.

129. Rossolimo-Wood, Hastings 1949/50
1 f4!! ♖ba7 (on *1...gxf4* White had prepared *2 g5! fxg5 3 ♕h3+!*) 2 ♕h3 ♕d8 3 fxg5 fxg5 4 ♖c1 ♕e7 5 ♕c3! ♕d8 6 ♖f1! ♘e7 7 ♖f5! ♖d7 8 ♕xe5+! Black resigns (*8...dxe5 9 ♖e6* mate).

130. Klaman-Genin, Leningrad, 1962
1...♕h8! 2 ♖h2 (forced, since *2...♖h6!* was threatened) 2...♕xh2+!! 3 ♔xh2 ♖h8+ 4 ♔g1 ♖gh6 5 gxf4 ♖h1+ 6 ♔g2 ♖8h2+ 7 ♔g3 ♗h3 8 ♖b2 ♖xb2, and Black won. The game concluded 9 ♗d2 ♘f6 10 ♔f2 ♘h5 11 ♕xc5 ♖h2+ 12 ♔e3 ♘xf4 White resigns.

131. Sigurjonsson-Vizantiades, Skopje, 1972
1...♖xf3! 2 ♕xd5 ♖h3+!! 3 gxh3 ♗xd5+ 4 ♔h2 ♗e5 mate.

132. Kellerman-Freidl, Nuremberg, 1955
1...♕f6+ 2 ♘f3 (if *2 ♘f5 ♗e3!*) 2...♗e3+ 3 ♔f1 ♕xf3+! 4 gxf3 ♗h3 mate.

133. White to play (7 mins.)

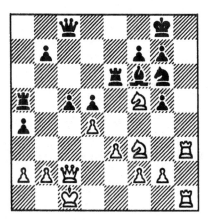

134. Black to play (8 mins.)

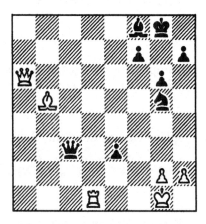

135. White to play (10 mins.)

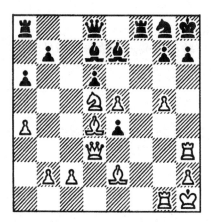

136. Black to play (6 mins.)

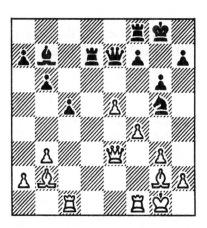

137. White to play (8 mins.)

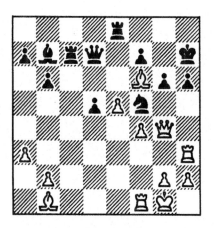

138. White to play (10 mins.)

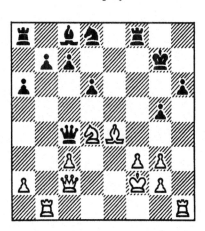

SOLUTIONS TO POSITIONS 133-138

133. Kampfhenkel-Palmstet, Vienna, 1961
1 ♘e7+!! ♗xe7 2 ♖h8+!! ♘xh8 3 ♕h7+ ♔f8 4 ♕xh8 mate.

134. Spiers-Davey, London, 1950
1...e2!! 2 ♗xe2 ♕e3+ 3 ♔h1 *(3 ♔f1 is decisively met by 3... ♘e4!)* 3...♘h3! 4
gxh3 ♕e4+ 5 ♔g1 ♗c5+ White resigns.

135. Tukmakov-Panno, Buenos Aires, 1970
1 e6! exd3 *(or 1...♗xe6 2 ♗xg7+ ♔xg7 3 ♕d4+ ♔f7 4 ♘h5 mate)* 2 ♗xd3 ♘f6 3
gxf6 ♗xf6 4 ♖xh7+ ♔g8 5 ♘xf6+ Black resigns.

136. Reicher-Mititelu, Bucharest, 1952 (variation)
1...♗xg2 2 ♔xg2 ♖d2+! 3 ♕xd2 *(if 3 ♖f2 ♕b7+ 4 ♔g1 ♘h3+ 5 ♔f1 ♕h1 mate)*
3...♕b7+ 4 ♔g1 *(or 4 ♔f2 ♘e4+)* 4...♘h3 mate.

137. Lipnitsky-Sidorov, Riga, 1954
1 ♖h5! ♘g7 *(if 1... ♖g8 2 ♖xf5 gxf5 3 ♗xf5+ ♖g6 4 ♗xd7 ♖xg4 5 ♗xg4)* 2
♖xh6+! ♔xh6 3 ♕h4+ ♘h5 4 ♕g5+ ♔h7 5 ♕xh5+ Black resigns.

138. Balayev-Ilyazov, Ordzhonikidze, 1974
1 ♖xh6! ♔xh6 2 ♖h1+ ♔g7 3 ♗d5!! ♕xd5 4 ♕h7+ ♔f6 5 ♖h6+ ♔e5 6 ♕g7+
Black resigns.

139. Black to play (12 mins.)

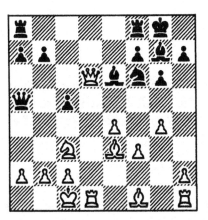

140. White to play (14 mins.)

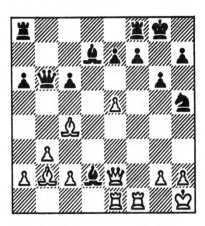

141. Black to play (10 mins.)

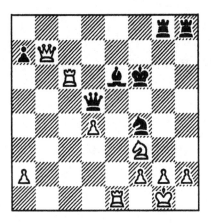

142. White to play (15 mins.)

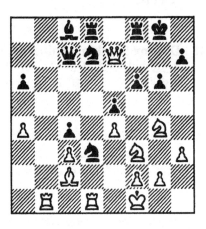

143. White to play (18 mins.)

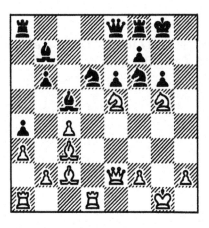

144. White to play (15 mins.)

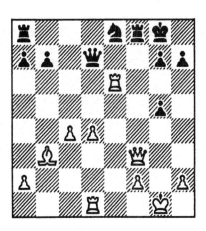

SOLUTIONS TO POSITIONS 139-144

139. Steiner-Zhukovitsky, Sevastopol, 1968
1...♘xe4!! 2 fxe4 (no better is *2 ♘xe4 ♕xa2 3 ♕xc5 ♕xb2+ 4 ♔d2 ♖ac8, or 3 ♗d3 ♕xb2+ 4 ♔d2 ♖fd8 5 ♕xc5 ♖ac8 6 ♖b1 ♕a2*) 2...♗xc3 3 ♕xc5 (*3 bxc3 fails to 3...♕a3+ 4 ♔b1 ♗xa2+*) 3...♗xb2+! 4 ♔xb2 ♕xa2+ 5 ♔c1 ♖fc8 6 ♗c4 ♗xc4 White resigns.

140. Andersen-Vaier, Denmark, 1969
1 e6!! ♗xe6 (or *1... ♗xe1 2 exf7+ ♖xf7 3 ♕xe7 ♖af8 4 ♕e5!*) 2 ♕xe6!! (*2 ♗xe6 is met by 2...♗xe1, but now this would fail to 3 ♖xf7; it is equally bad to accept the sacrifice: 2...fxe6 3 ♗xe6+ ♖f7 4 ♖xf7 ♘f6 5 ♖xf6+ ♔g7 6 ♖f7+ ♔h6 7 ♗g7+ ♔h5 8 ♖e4!*) 2...♘g7 3 ♕e5 ♗h6 4 ♕xe7 ♖a7 5 ♖xf7! ♖xf7 6 ♗xf7+ Black resigns.

141. Dyaltov-Shashin, Leningrad, 1962
1...♖xg2+ 2 ♔f1 (or *2 ♔h1 ♖gxh2+ 3 ♔g1 ♖h1 mate*) 2...♖g1+!! 3 ♔xg1 ♖g8+ 4 ♔f1 ♕c4+!! 5 ♖xc4 ♗h3 mate.

142. Keres-Gligoric, Zurich, 1959
1 ♖xd3 cxd3 2 ♗b3+ ♔h8 3 ♘xf6!! ♖xf6 4 ♘g5 ♖xf2+! 5 ♔g1 (not *5 ♔xf2 ♕c5+!*) 5...♖f1+ 6 ♔h2 Black resigns.

143. Hecht-Keene, West Germany, 1966
1 ♘d7!! ♕xd7 (or *1...♘xd7 2 ♕h5!*) 2 ♗xf6 ♕c6 3 ♖d5!! exd5 4 ♕h5! ♗xf2+ 5 ♔xf2 ♘e4+ 6 ♘xe4 gxh5 7 ♖g1+ ♔h7 8 ♘c5+ Black resigns.

144. Janosevic-Danov, Skopje, 1961
1 c5!! ♖f7 (if *1... ♖xf3 2 ♖xe8 mate*) 2 ♕xf7+! ♔xf7 (or *2... ♕xf7 3 ♖e7!*) 3 ♖d6+ ♔e7 4 ♖e1+ ♔d8 5 ♖xd7+ ♔xd7 6 ♗a4+ Black resigns.

145. White to play (10 mins.)

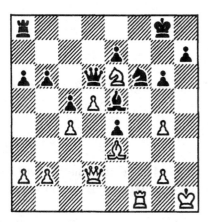

146. White to play (12 mins.)

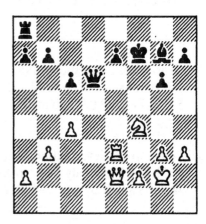

147. White to play (18 mins.)

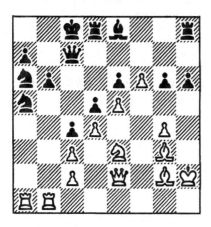

148. Black to play (15 mins.)

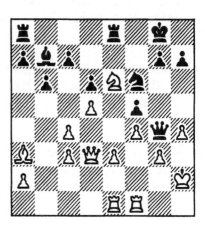

149. White to play (15 mins.)

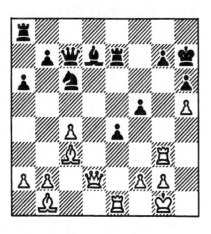

150. White to play (20 mins.)

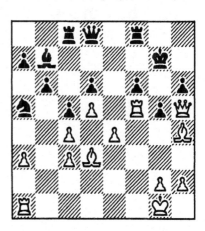

SOLUTIONS TO POSITIONS 145-150

145. Graf-Wurm, Augsburg, 1953
1 ♗xc5! bxc5 2 ♕h6 ♘d7 3 ♖f7!! ♔xf7 4 ♕xh7+ ♗g7 (or *4... ♔f6 5 ♕g7 mate*)
5 ♕xg7+ ♔e8 6 ♕xg6 mate.

146. Lein-Lavrentiev, Arkhangelsk, 1959
1 c5! ♕xc5 (the only move to prevent the check at c4 and defend the e-pawn) 2 b4!
♕xb4 3 a3! ♕d6 4 ♕a2+! ♔e8 5 ♕g8+ ♗f8 6 ♘e6 ♕d5+ 7 ♖f3, and White won.

147. Suetin-Bagirov, Minsk, 1961
1 ♘xd5!! exd5 2 e6 ♘c6 3 ♖xa5!! bxa5 4 ♕e5! ♕c7 (on *4... ♘c7* White wins by
either *5 e7* or *5 ♗b5!*) 5 ♗xd5! ♖xd5 (*5... ♕xe5* fails to *6 ♗b7+*) 6 ♕xd5 ♕c6 7
♕xa5! Black resigns. There is no defence against 8 ♕xa6+.

148. Malcanek-Teschner, Reggio Emilia 1964/65
1... ♖xe6!! 2 dxe6 ♘e4 3 ♖g1 ♘xg3! 4 e4 (*4 ♖xg3 ♕xh4+ 5 ♖h3 ♕f2 mate, or 5*
♔g1 ♕xg3+) 4... ♕xh4+ 5 ♔g2 ♘xe4 6 ♕e3 ♘d2+ White resigns.

149. Lindner-Forgacs, Budapest, 1953
1 ♖xe4!! fxe4 2 ♗xe4+ ♔g8 3 ♖xh6 ♗e6 (White was threatening not only *4*
♖xg7+, but also *4 ♗d5+*) 4 ♕h7+ ♔f8 5 ♕h8+ ♗g8 6 ♗d5 ♖f7 7 ♗xf7 ♕xf7 8
♖f3 Black resigns.

150. Kashits-Polyakov, USSR, 1950
1 e5!! (threatening *2 ♖xg5+*) 1... ♕e8 2 exf6+ ♖xf6 3 ♖xg5+ hxg5 4 ♕h7+ ♔f8 5
♗xg5 ♕f7 6 ♕h8+ ♔e7 7 ♗xf6+ ♕xf6 8 ♖e1+ ♔f7 9 ♕h7+ ♔f8 10 ♖f1 Black
resigns.

Theme: "Utilization of open diagonals" (Nos. 151-156)

151. White to play (6 mins.)

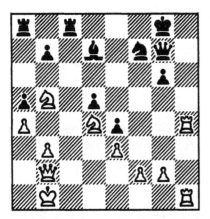

152. Black to play (10 mins.)

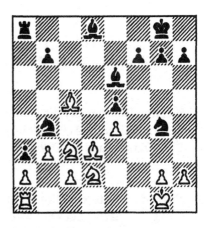

153. White to play (7 mins.)

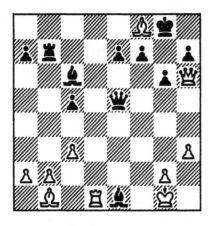

154. White to play (6 mins.)

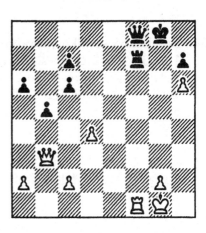

155. White to play (6 mins.)

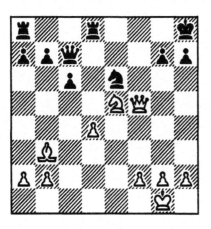

156. Black to play (12 mins.)

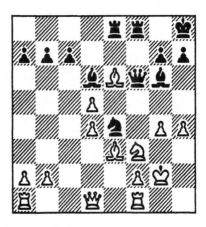

SOLUTIONS TO POSITIONS 151-156

151. Ljubisavlevic-Albano, La Speci, 1973
1 ♘d6! ♘xd6 2 ♖h8+ ♕xh8 3 ♖xh8+ ♔xh8 4 ♘e6+ ♔h7 5 ♕g7+ mate.

152. Sterner-Boleslavsky, Stockholm, 1954
1...♘xd3 2 cxd3 ♖c8! 3 ♗b4 ♗b6+ 4 ♔f1 (on *4 ♔h1* there follows *4... ♘f2+ 5 ♔g1 ♘xd3+* and *6... ♗xb4*) 4...♘e3+ 5 ♔e2 ♘c2 White resigns.

153. Bartrina-Ghitescu, Olot, 1974
1 ♗g7! (*1 ♖d8?* does not work, on account of *1... ♗f2+*) 1...♗f2+ (*1...♔xg7 2 ♖d8+*) 2 ♔f1 (not *2 ♔xf2 ♖xb2+*, or *2 ♔h1 ♗xg2+!*) 2...♗b5+ (*2...♕b8* loses to *3 ♗e5!!*) 3 ♔xf2 ♕e2+ 4 ♔g3 ♕xd1 5 ♗h8!! ♕d6+ 6 ♔f2 Black resigns.

154. Damjanovic-Lutikov, Sarajevo, 1969 (variation)
1 ♕g3+ ♔h8 2 ♕e5+ ♔g8 3 ♕g5+! ♔h8 4 ♖xf7! ♕xf7 5 ♕d8+ ♔g8 6 ♕f6+ and mate next move. In the game White overlooked this possibility, and after 1 ♕e6 ♕e7 2 ♕g4+ ♔f8 3 ♕c8+ ♕e8 4 ♖xf7+ ♔xf7 5 ♕xc7+ ♔g6 the players agreed a draw.

155. Rabar-Bajec, Sarajevo, 1951
1 ♘g6+!! hxg6 2 ♕h3+ ♔g8 3 ♕xe6+ ♔f8 4 ♕g8+ ♔e7 5 ♕f7+ ♔d6 6 ♕e6 mate.

156. Norman-Hansen v. Andersen, Copenhagen, 1954
1...♖xe6!! 2 dxe6 ♘c3! 3 bxc3 ♗e4 4 ♔h3 ♕xf3+ 5 ♕xf3 ♖xf3+ 6 ♔g2 ♖g3+ 7 ♔h2 ♖g2+ 8 ♔h1 ♖h2+ 9 ♔g1 ♖h1 mate.

Theme: "Smothered mate" (Nos. 157-162)

157. Black to play (10 mins.)

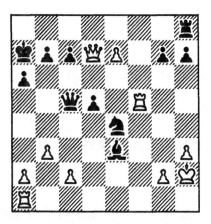

158. White to play (8 mins.)

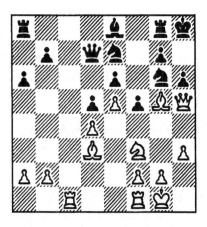

159. Black to play (8 mins.)

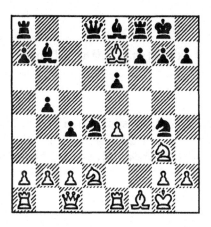

160. Black to play (12 mins.)

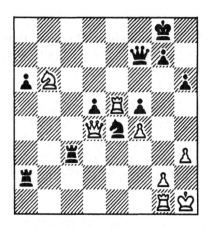

161. White to play (5 mins.)

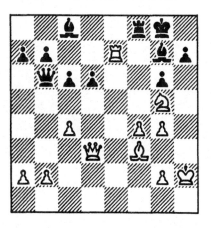

162. Black to play (12 mins.)

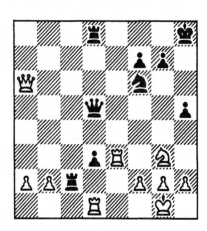

SOLUTIONS TO POSITIONS 57-162

157. Sapunov-Bobotsov, Plovdiv, 1949
1...♖e8!! 2 ♖xd5 (or *2 ♕xe8 ♕d6+ 3 ♔h1 ♘g3+ 4 ♔h2 ♘f1+ 5 ♔h1 ♕h2* mate) 2...♗f4+ 3 ♔h1 ♘f2+ 4 ♔g1 ♘xh3+ 5 ♔h1 ♕g1+! 6 ♖xg1 ♘f2 mate.

158. Khanov-Pozdeyev, Ashkhabad, 1951
1 ♗f6! ♘f8 2 ♕xh6+ ♔h7 3 ♘g5 ♗g6 4 ♕xh7+! ♗xh7 5 ♘f7 mate.

159. Kandolin-Ojanen, Helsinki, 1963
1...♕b6!! 2 ♔h1 (played to avert the threat of *2... ♘f3+* or *2... ♘e2+ 3 ♔h1 ♘f2* mate, but insufficient, as the course of the game shows) 2...♘f2+ 3 ♔g1 ♘e2+! 4 ♘xe2 ♘h3+ 5 ♔h1 ♕g1+ 6 ♘xg1 ♘f2 mate.

160. Larsen-Najdorf, Lugano, 1968
1...♕h5!! 2 ♕xd5+ ♔h7 3 ♕xa2 ♖xh3+!! 4 gxh3 ♕xh3+ 5 ♕h2 ♘f2 mate.

161. Zgurev-Mechkarov, Sofia, 1949 (variation)
1 ♗d5+!! cxd5 (in the game Black played *1... ♔h8*, but resigned after *2 ♕c3!!*, since if *2... ♖g8 3 ♘f7* mate, *2...♗xc3 3 ♖xh7* mate, or *2...♕d4 3 ♕xd4*) 2 ♕xd5+ ♔h8 3 ♘f7+ ♔g8 (Black is mated after *3... ♖xf7 4 ♕xf7 ♕d4 5 ♖e8+*) 4 ♘h6+ ♔h8 5 ♕g8+ ♖xg8 6 ♘f7 mate.

162. Evans-Larsen, Dallas, 1958
1...♖xf2!! 2 ♘e4 (*2 ♔xf2 ♘g4+*) 2...♘xe4 3 ♖exd3 ♖f1+!! 4 ♖xf1 (or *4 ♔xf1 ♕f5+ 5 ♔g1 ♕c5+!*) 4...♕c5+ White resigns. Black has a smothered mate.

Theme: "Blocking" (Nos. 163-164)

163. White to play (8 mins.)

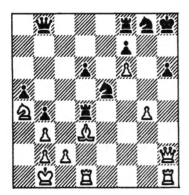

164. White to play (12 mins.)

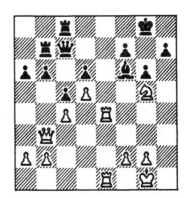

Theme: "X-ray" (Nos. 165-166)

165. White to play (7 mins.)

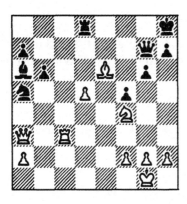

166. Black to play (10 mins.)

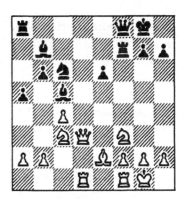

Theme: "Overloading" (Nos. 167-174)

167. White to play (6 mins.)

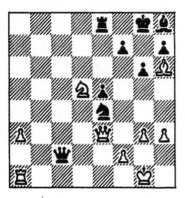

168. Black to play (8 mins.)

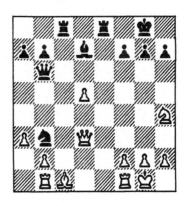

SOLUTIONS TO POSITIONS 163-168

163. Janke-Gawlikowski, Warsaw, 1959
1 ♕xh6+!! ♘xh6 2 ♖xh6+ ♔g8 3 ♖dh1 ♘g6 4 ♖h8+!! ♘xh8 5 ♗h7 mate.

164. Salminsh-Dagne, Corr., 1960/62
1 ♘xh7!! ♗g7 (other bishop moves would have been answered in the same way, while if *1... ♕d8 2 ♖e8+!*) 2 ♘f6+!! ♗xf6 3 ♖e8+ ♖xe8 4 ♖xe8+ ♔g7 5 ♕h3 g5 6 ♖h8! Black resigns.

165. Furman-Smyslov, Moscow, 1949
1 ♕b2!! ♘c4 (against the threat of *2 ♘xg6+* there is no satisfactory defence) 2 ♘xg6+! ♕xg6 3 ♖xc4+ ♕g7 4 ♕xg7+ ♔xg7 5 ♖c7+ Black resigns.

166. Euwe-Lundin, Zurich, 1952
1...♘e5!! 2 ♕c2 (or *2 ♘xe5 ♖xf2!!*) 2...♖xf3! 3 ♗xf3 ♘xf3+ 4 gxf3 (or *4 ♔h1 ♕f4! 5 g3 ♕h6!*) 4...♕xf3 5 ♘d5 ♕g4+ 6 ♔h1 exd5 7 f3 dxc4! White resigns.

167. Vranek-Mista, Prague, 1957
1 ♖c1 ♕a4 2 ♕xe4!! ♕xe4 3 ♘e7+! ♖xe7 4 ♖c8+ ♖e8 5 ♖xe8 mate.

168. Rudakovsky-Botvinnik, Moscow, 1945 (variation)
1...♘xc1 2 ♖bxc1 ♖xc1 3 ♖xc1 ♕h6!! 4 ♕c4 ♗b5! 5 ♕c5 b6, and Black wins.

169. White to play (10 mins.)

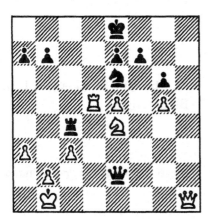

170. White to play (8 mins.)

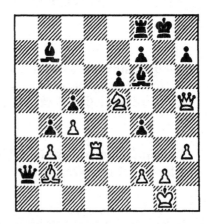

171. White to play (7 mins.)

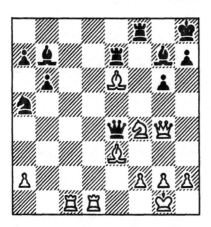

172. Black to play (7 mins.)

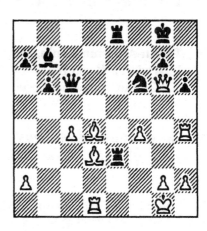

173. White to play (6 mins.)

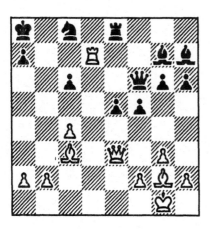

174. White to play (16 mins.)

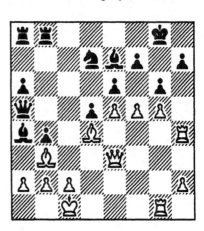

SOLUTIONS TO POSITIONS 169-174

169. Djindjihashvili-Tukmakov, Leningrad, 1971
1 ♞c5!! ♖f4 (no better is *1... ♖xc5 2 ♕h8+ ♞f8 3 ♖xc5*) 2 ♕h8+ ♞f8 3 ♖d8+!
♔xd8 4 ♕xf8+ ♔c7 5 ♕xe7+ ♔c6 6 ♕xb7+ Black resigns.

170. Tseitlin-Gulko, Novosibirsk, 1971
1 ♖d8!! ♕b1+ 2 ♔h2 ♗xd8 3 ♕g4+ ♕g6 4 ♞xg6 hxg6 5 ♕xf4, and White won.

171. Geller-Kapengut, Leningrad, 1971
1 ♖d4!! ♖xf4 (if *1...♗xd4 2 ♗xd4+ ♕xd4 3 ♞xg6+*, or *1...♕e5 2 ♞xg6+ and 3
♕h4+*) 2 ♖d8+! ♖f8 (on *2...♗f8* there follows *3 ♖xf8+ ♖xf8 4 ♗d4+ ♖g7 5
♕xe4 ♗xe4 6 ♖c7!*) 3 ♖xf8+ ♗xf8 4 ♕xe4 Black resigns.

172. Tolush-Antoshin, Leningrad, 1956
1...♖xd3!! 2 ♖xd3 ♖e1+ 3 ♔f2 ♞e4+ 4 ♔xe1 ♕xg6, and Black won. 1...♖e2? 2
♗xe2 ♖xe2 would have been weaker in view of 3 ♖g4!

173. Smyslov-Euwe, Zurich, 1953 (variation)
1 ♗xe5!! ♖xe5 2 ♕xe5! ♕xe5 3 ♗xc6+ ♔b8 4 ♖b7+ ♔a8 5 ♖b5 mate.

174. Velimirovic-Fridjonsson, Reykjavik, 1974
1 fxe6 fxe6 2 ♕h3 ♞f8 3 ♖xh7! ♞xh7 (if *3...♗xb3 4 ♖h8+ ♔f7 5 ♖f1+ ♔e8 6
♖fxf8+ ♗xf8 7 ♕xe6+ ♔d8 8 ♖xf8+ ♔c7 9 ♖f7+*) 4 ♕xe6+ ♔f8 (bad is
4...♔h8 5 ♕xe7 and 6 e6+) 5 ♖f1+ ♔e8 6 ♖f7! ♖b7 7 ♗xa4+ ♕xa4 8 ♖xh7
♔d8 9 ♗b6+! ♖xb6 10 ♕xe7+ Black resigns.

Theme: "Exploiting a back rank weakness" (Nos. 175-192)

175. White to play (5 mins.)

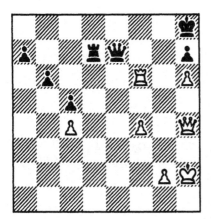

176. Black to play (10 mins.)

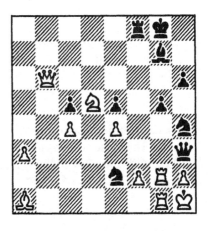

177. White to play (7 mins.)

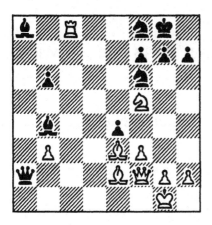

178. White to play (9 mins.)

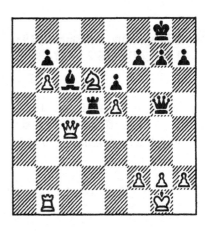

179. Black to play (10 mins.)

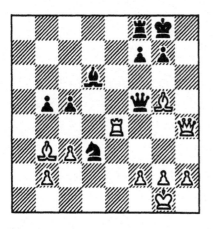

180. White to play (7 mins.)

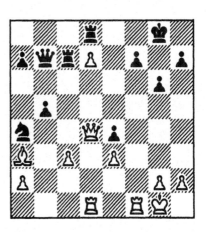

SOLUTIONS TO POSITIONS 175-180

175. Koshnitsky-Wolfer, Adelaide, 1972
1 ♕e1! ♕d8 (if *1... ♔g8 2 ♖e6!!*) 2 ♕e5! ♔g8 3 ♕e6+ ♔h8 4 ♕xd7! Black resigns.

176. Torre-Radulov, Leningrad, 1973
1...♕f3! (White still has chances of resisting after *1... ♘xg1 2 ♖g3 ♕f1 3 ♖xg1 ♖xf2 4 ♕e6+ ♔h7 5 ♕g4*) 2 ♕e6+ ♔h7 3 ♕g4 ♘xg1 4 ♔xg1 (or *4 ♕xf3 ♘gxf3*) 4...♖b8!! 5 ♘c3 ♕xc3! White resigns.

177. Osnos-Dely, Budapest, 1965
1 ♗c5!! ♗xc5 2 ♕xc5! ♘6d7 3 ♕xf8+!! ♘xf8 4 ♘e7+ ♔h8 5 ♖xf8 mate.

178. Sliwa-Stoltz, Bucharest, 1953
1 ♕xc6!! bxc6 2 b7 ♕d8 3 b8Q ♖d1+ 4 ♖xd1 ♕xb8 5 ♘b7!!, and White won.

179. Vikman-Iovcic, Corr., 1955
1...♗f4!! 2 ♖xf4 ♘xf4 3 ♕xf4 ♕b1+ 4 ♕c1 ♕xc1+ 5 ♗xc1 ♖a8! White resigns (there is no defence against *6... ♖a1*).

180. Corning-Sherwood, Corr., 1963
1 ♕f6! ♖dxd7 2 ♕d8+! ♖xd8 3 ♖xd8+ ♔g7 4 ♗f8+ ♔g8 5 ♗h6 mate.

181. White to play (10 mins.)

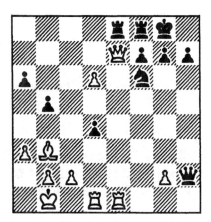

182. Black to play (10 mins.)

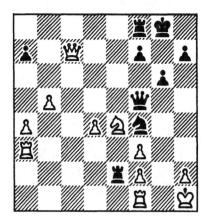

183. White to play (15 mins.)

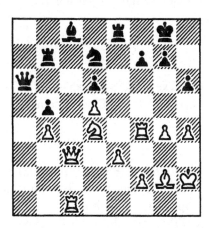

184. White to play (16 mins.)

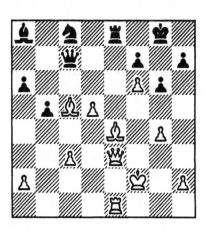

185. Black to play (20 mins.)

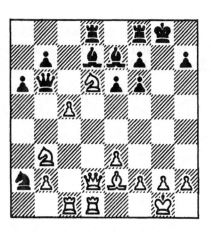

186. White to play (20 mins.)

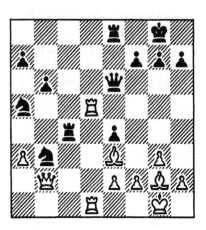

SOLUTIONS TO POSITIONS 181-186

181. Velimirovic-Csom, Amsterdam, 1974
1 ♗xf7+!! ♖xf7 2 ♕xe8+! ♘xe8 3 ♖xe8+ ♖f8 4 d7 ♕d6 5 ♖f1!! Black resigns.

182. Spiridonov-Krogius, Sochi, 1973 (variation)
1...♖c8! 2 ♕e5 ♕h3 3 ♖g1 ♕g2+!! 4 ♖xg2 ♖c1+ 5 ♖g1 ♖xg1+ 6 ♔xg1 ♖e1
mate. In the game Black missed this possibility, and played 1...♖xe4 2 fxe4 ♕xe4+
3 f3 ♕e2 4 ♖g1 ♘d3 5 ♖xd3 ♕xd3, but in the end he still managed to win.

183. Horowitz-Denker, New York, 1946
1 ♕xc8! ♖xc8 2 ♖xc8+ ♘f8 (if *2...♔h7 3 ♗e4+ g6 4 ♖xf7* mate) 3 ♘e6! fxe6 4
♖fxf8+ ♔h7 5 ♗e4+ g6 6 ♖h8+ ♔g7 7 g5! Black resigns. Against 8 ♖cg8+ ♔f7
9 ♗xg6+ and 10 ♖h7+ there is no defence.

184. Dely-Hajtun, Budapest, 1954
1 ♕h6!! ♕xc5+ 2 ♖e3 ♕f8 3 ♗xg6! ♕xh6 4 ♖xe8+ ♕f8 5 ♗xh7+! ♔xh7 6
♖xf8 ♗xd5 (*6...♘b6 7 ♖b8*, or *6...♗b7 7 ♖xf7+*) 7 ♖xc8 Black resigns.

185. Szabo-Korchnoi, Lugano, 1968
1...♕xb3!! 2 ♗c4 ♘xc1 (after *2...♕a4 3 ♖a1* White has the better position) 3
♗xb3 ♘xb3 4 ♕b4 (White thought that, on account of this move, the entire combination was not possible, but an unpleasant surprise awaited him) 4...♘xc5!! 5
♕xc5 ♗a4! 6 b3 (if *6 ♖d2 ♗xd6 7 ♖xd6 ♖c8!*) 6...♗xb3 7 ♖d3 ♗d5! 8 e4
♗xe4 White resigns.

186. Makogonov-Smyslov, Moscow, 1940
1 ♖e5!! ♕c8 (or *1...♕xe5 2 ♕xe5 ♖xe5 3 ♖d8+*, and wins) 2 ♘h3! ♖d8 (if
2...♕b8 3 ♖g5 g6 4 ♖b5, threatening both *5 ♖xb3* and *5 ♗h6!*) 3 ♗xc8 ♖xd1+ 4
♔g2 ♖xc8 5 ♖g5 g6 6 ♖b5 (or *6 ♖xa5 ♘xa5 7 ♗h6*) 6...♖d6 7 ♖xb3 ♘xb3 8
♕xb3 Black resigns.

187. White to play (16 mins.)

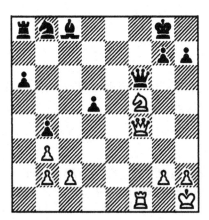

188. White to play (18 mins.)

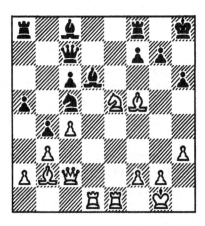

189. Black to play (12 mins.)

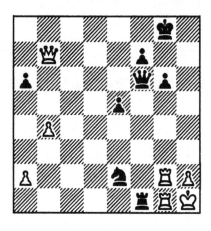

190. Black to play (8 mins.)

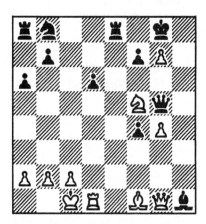

191. White to play (10 mins.)

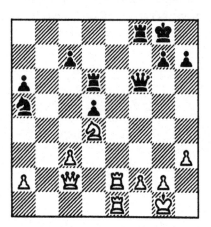

192. White to play (25 mins.)

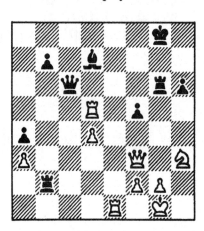

SOLUTIONS TO POSITIONS 187-192

187. Liboreito-Link, Argentina, 1969
1 ♘h6+! ♔h8 2 ♕c1! ♕e7 3 ♕g5 ♕e8 4 ♘f7+ ♔g8 5 ♘d6 ♕d7 6 ♕xd5+ ♕e6
7 ♘xc8 ♕xd5 8 ♘e7+ ♔h8 9 ♖f8+ Black resigns.

188. Gheorghiu-Kinmark, The Hague, 1961
1 ♖xd6!! ♕xd6 (or *1... ♗xf5 2 ♖xh6+! gxh6 3 ♘xf7+ ♔g8 4 ♘xh6+*, and wins) 2
♘xf7+!! ♖xf7 3 ♖e8+ ♕f8 (*3... ♖f8 loses immediately to 4 ♕d2!!*) 4 ♖xf8+
♖xf8 5 ♕d2 ♔g8 6 ♕d4! ♖f7 7 ♗xc8 ♖xc8 8 ♕xc5 ♖cf8 9 ♗d4 Black resigns.

189. Prins-Soultanbiev, Hastings 1949/50
1...♕f2! 2 ♕c8+ ♔g7 3 ♕c5 ♖xg1+ 4 ♖xg1 ♕f3+ 5 ♖g2 ♕f1+ 6 ♖g1 ♘g3+!!
7 hxg3 ♕h3 mate.

190. Golbin-Vetemaa, Gomel 1973
1...f3+ 2 ♔b1 ♕d2! 3 ♗c4 f2 4 ♕xh1 ♕xd1+!! 5 ♕xd1 ♖e1, and Black won.

191. Tseshkovsky-Semenyuk, Chelyabinsk, 1975
1 ♘e6! ♖c8 2 ♘xc7! ♖xc7 3 ♖e8+ ♔f7 4 ♕xh7 ♖cc6 5 ♖f8+!! Black resigns
(*5... ♔xf8 6 ♕h8+ ♔f7 7 ♕e8 mate*).

192. Estrin-Zapletal, 7th World Corr. Ch., 1972-76
1 ♖e7! ♖b3 2 ♕xf5! (not *2 ♖dxd7 ♕xd7 3 ♕xb3+ axb3 4 ♖xd7 ♖b6*, when the
passed b-pawn cannot be stopped) 2...♕c1+ (*2... ♗xf5 3 ♖d8 mate*, while if
2... ♖xg2+ 3 ♔f1!) 3 ♔h2 ♖xh3+! 4 ♕xh3 ♕f4+ 5 ♕g3!! (White loses after *5
♔g1 ♗xh3 6 ♖d8+ ♔f8, or 5 g3 ♕xf2+ 6 ♕g2 ♕xg2+ 7 ♔xg2 ♗c6*) 5...♖xg3 6
fxg3 ♕g4 7 ♖exd7! Black resigns.

Theme: "Weakness of the second rank" (Nos. 193-198)

193. White to play (6 mins.)

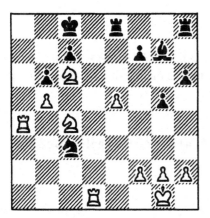

194. Black to play (12 mins.)

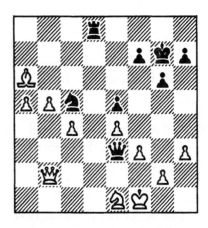

195. Black to play (10 mins.)

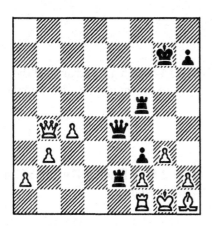

196. White to play (8 mins.)

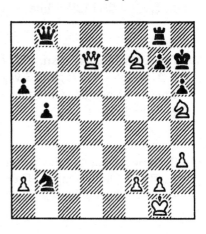

197. Black to play (8 mins.)

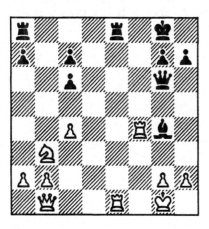

198. White to play (12 mins.)

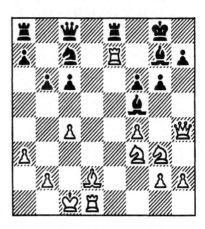

SOLUTIONS TO POSITIONS 193-198

193. Galik-Hodak, Budva, 1958
1 ♖a8+ ♔b7 2 ♖a7+ ♔c8 3 ♘d6+! cxd6 (or *3...♔d7 4 ♘xe8+ ♘xd1 5 ♘xg7*) 4 exd6 Black resigns. There is no defence against the mating threats of 5 ♖c7 and 5 d7.

194. Weiss-Komponovo, Zurich, 1954
1...♖d2! 2 ♕xe5+ ♔h6 3 ♕g3 ♘xe4!! 4 ♕h4+ ♔g7 5 fxe4 g5!! 6 ♘c2 ♕e2+ White resigns.

195. Bertok-Tolush, Vienna, 1957
1...♖xf2!! 2 ♕c3+ (*2 ♖xf2 ♕b1+ 3 ♖f1 f2+! 4 ♔g2 ♕e4+*, or *2 ♔xf2 ♕d4+ 3 ♔e1 ♕e5 mate*) 2...♔g6 3 ♖e1 (or *3 ♔xf2 ♕e2+ 4 ♔g1 f2+ 5 ♔g2 ♕e4+*) 3...♖e2! 4 ♔f1 f2!! White resigns.

196. Tal-Antoshin, Yerevan, 1957 (variation)
1 ♕f5+! g6 2 ♕d7! gxh5 3 ♘g5+ ♔g6 4 ♕e6+!! ♔xg5 5 g3, and against the threats of 6 h4+ and 6 f4+ there is no defence. White in fact played 1 h4, and the game ended in a draw.

197. Bredewout-Karaklajic, Beverwijk, 1967
1...♖e2!! (threatening *2... ♖xg2+ 3 ♔xg2 ♗f5+*) 2 ♖f2 ♖ae8 3 ♖ef1 ♖xf2 4 ♔xf2 ♖e2+ 5 ♔g1 ♖xg2+! 6 ♔h1 ♖g1+! White resigns.

198. Ljubojevic-Donner, Wijk aan Zee, 1973
1 ♘xf5 gxf5 2 ♖xg7+! ♔xg7 3 ♗c3 ♖e6 (or *3... ♖f8 4 ♕g5+*) 4 ♘g5! h6 5 ♘xe6+ ♕xe6 6 ♖e1 ♕f7 7 ♗xf6+ ♔g6 (or *7...♕xf6 8 ♖e7+ ♔g6 9 ♕g3+*, and wins) 8 ♖e7 ♕xc4+ 9 ♗c3 Black resigns.

Theme: "Intermediate move" (Nos. 199-202)

199. Black to play (10 mins.)
Black to move reckoned that he could capture the e4 pawn "for free". What had he overlooked?

200. White to play (6 mins.)
Black, of course, took into account the possible double attack 1 ♕h3, but thought that after 1...♗xd5 he would parry the threats. What had he missed?

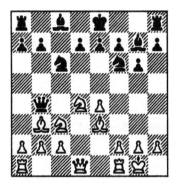

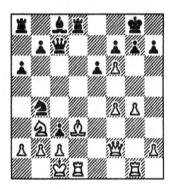

201. Black to play (16 mins.)
White has just played e4-e5, confident that the e-pawn is invulnerable, since if 1...♘xe5 2 ♗xe5 ♕xe5 3 ♖e1 is decisive. Black, however, thought differently...

202. White to play (20 mins.)
Both players saw the combination beginning with 1 ♗xh7+, but assessed its correctness differently.

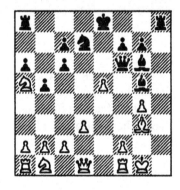

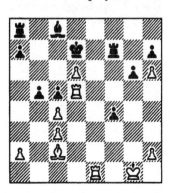

Theme: "Creation and utilization of passed pawns" (Nos. 203-226)

203. White to play (5 mins.)

204. White to play (7 mins.)

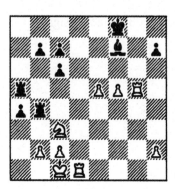

SOLUTIONS TO POSITIONS 199-204

199. Grambczevski-Filep, Lublin, 1967

1...♘xe4?? 2 ♘xc6! bxc6 3 a3 ♘xc3 4 ♕f3!! ♕xb3 (no better is *4... ♘e2+ 5 ♔h1! ♕h4 6 ♕xf7+ ♔d8 7 ♕xg7 ♕f6 8 ♕xf6 exf6 9 ♗c4*, when White wins a piece) 5 cxb3 Black resigns.

200. Mukhin-Chechelian, Moscow, 1972

1 ♕h3 ♗xd5 2 ♗b5+!! ♔f8 (*2...♔d8 3 ♕d7* mate) 3 ♕xh6+ ♔g8 4 exd5 f5 (if *4...♕xb5, 5 ♖d3!* is decisive) 5 ♗d7 Black resigns.

201. Nippgen-Werhegen, Strasbourg, 1973

1...♘xe5! 2 ♖xe5 ♗e4!! 3 f4 (on *3 dxe4 ♕xe5 4 ♖e1* Black had prepared *4...♕h2+ 5 ♔f1 ♕h1+ 6 ♔e2 ♕xe4+*) 3...♕xe5! 4 dxe4 ♗xf4 5 ♕f3 (if *5 ♕e2 ♖h2*) 5...♗e3+ 6 ♖f2 ♕h2+ 7 ♔f1 ♗xf2 8 ♕xf2 ♕h1+ 9 ♔e2 ♕xe4+ White resigns.

202. Spassky-Capelan, Solingen, 1974

1 ♗xh7+! ♔xh7 2 ♕h4+ ♔g8 3 ♕g5! ♖xd1+ 4 ♖xd1 cxb2+ 5 ♔xb2 ♕xc2+ 6 ♔a3 ♕g6 (it was on this move that Black was pinning his hopes, but...) 7 ♖d8+ ♔h7 8 ♕h4+ ♕h6 9 fxg7!! (this was the move that Black had not foreseen) 9...♔xg7 10 ♖g8+ ♔xg8 11 ♕xh6, and White won. There followed 11...♘c6 12 ♘c5 ♘e7 13 ♘e4 ♘d5 14 g5, and Black resigned.

203. Peresipkin-Romanishin, Odessa, 1972

1 f6 ♔e8 2 e6!! ♖xg5 3 ♖d8+ ♔xd8 4 exf7 Black resigns.

204. Boey-Filip, Belgium, 1972

1 ♗xg6!! hxg6 2 ♖e7+! ♖xe7 3 dxe7+ ♔xe7 4 ♖d8!! Black resigns.

205. Black to play (10 mins.)

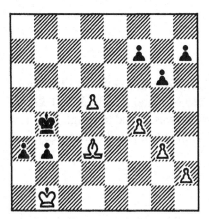

206. Black to play (12 mins.)

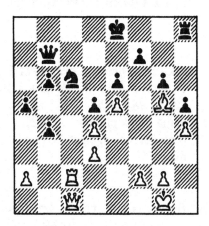

207. White to play (7 mins.)

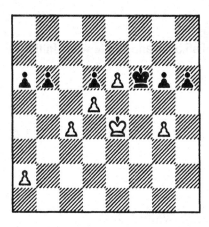

208. Black to play (8 mins.)

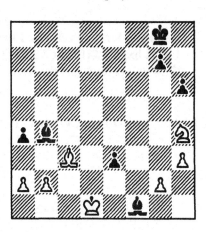

209. Black to play (10 mins.)

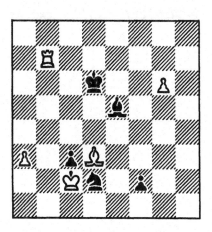

210. Black to play (8 mins.)

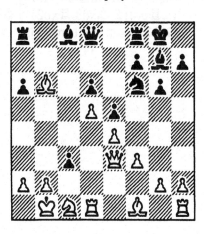

SOLUTIONS TO POSITIONS 205-210

205. Fiklni-Serbrnik, Corr., 1971/72
1...♔c3 2 ♗b5 (if *2 d6 a2+ 3 ♔a1 ♔xd3 4 ♔b2 a1=♕+ 5 ♔xa1 ♔c2, or 4 d7 ♔c2 5 d8=♕ b2+ 6 ♔xa2 b1=♕+ 7 ♔a3 ♕b3+ mate*) 2...a2+ 3 ♔a1 ♔b4! In the game Black played 3...♔c2?, and after 4 ♗a4 he was forced to resign. But now there is no defence against the two threats of 4...♔xb5, and 4...♔a3 followed by 5...b2 mate.

206. Barendregt-Portisch, Amsterdam, 1969
1...♘xd4!! 2 ♖c7 ♘e2+ 3 ♔f1 ♘xc1 4 ♖xb7 ♘xa2! 5 ♖b8+ ♔d7 White resigns. Only now did he see that after 6 ♖xh8 b3 7 ♖b8 b2 8 ♖xb6 ♘b4 Black gains a new queen.

207. Isakson-Morris, Pretoria, 1963 (variation)
1 g5+! hxg5 2 ♔f3 ♔e7 3 ♔g3 ♔f6 4 ♔g4 a5 5 a4, and White wins. In the game 1 ♔d4 was played, and the result was a draw.

208. Andreyev-Begun, Vitebsk, 1974
1...e2+ 2 ♔d2 (*2 ♔e1 would have been answered in the same way*) 2...a3! 3 ♗xb4 e1=♕+! 4 ♔xe1 axb2 White resigns.

209. Szabo-Kholmov, Leningrad, 1967
1...♘f3!! 2 g7 ♘e1+ 3 ♔b3 ♗xg7 4 ♖xg7 c2!! White resigns.

210. Jonsson-Kustinsson, Reykjavik, 1962
1...♖b8!! 2 ♗xd8 ♖xb2+ 3 ♔a1 c2 4 ♘b3 (*4 ♔xb2 cxd1=♘+!!*) 4...cxd1=♕+ 5 ♔xb2 ♖xd8 White resigns.

211. Black to play (10 mins.)

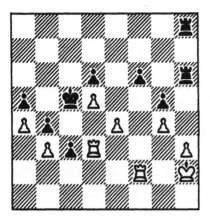

212. White to play (10 mins.)

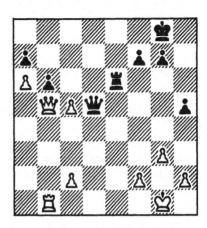

213. White to play (8 mins.)

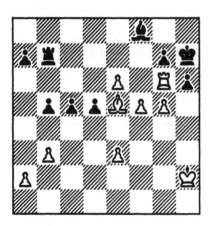

214. Black to play (7 mins.)

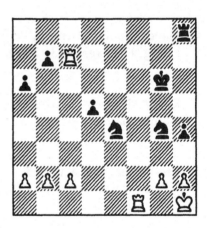

215. White to play (12 mins.)

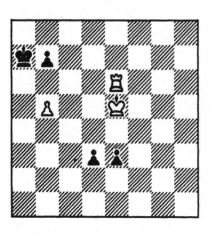

216. White to play (12 mins.)

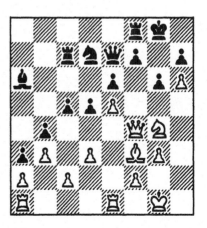

SOLUTIONS TO POSITIONS 211-216

211. Ajonen-Lahti, Helsinki, 1954
1...♖xh3+!! 2 ♖xh3 ♖xh3+ 3 ♔xh3 ♔d4 4 ♖xf6 c2 5 ♖f1 ♔xe4! White resigns.
The careless 5...♔d3?? would have reversed the result of the game after 6 e5!!

212. Smyslov-Guimard, Mar del Plata, 1962
1 cxb6!! ♖e1+ 2 ♖xe1 ♕xb5 3 bxa7 ♕c6 4 ♖b1! ♔h7 5 ♖b8 Black resigns.

213. Zurakhov-Zamykhovsky, Kiev, 1959
1 ♖xh6+!! gxh6 2 g6+ ♔g8 3 f6 ♗g7 4 e7! Black resigns. On 4...♖xe7 there follows 5 fxe7 ♗xe5+ 6 ♔h3.

214. Mandel-Johner, Genova, 1950
1...♘g3+! 2 hxg3 hxg3+ 3 ♔g1 ♘f2 4 ♖xf2 ♖h1+!! 5 ♔xh1 gxf2 White resigns.

215. Richter-Doronet, Berlin, 1949
1 ♔d6!! d2 2 ♔c7! d1=♕ 3 ♖a6+!! bxa6 4 b6+ ♔a8 5 b7+ ♔a7 6 b8=♕ mate.

216. Lee-Radulov, Sinaia, 1965
1 ♗xd5!! exd5 2 e6 ♘b6 3 ♕xc7!! ♕xc7 4 ♘f6+ ♔h8 5 e7 ♕b8 6 exf8=♕+
♕xf8 7 ♖e8, and White won.

217. White to play (15 mins.)

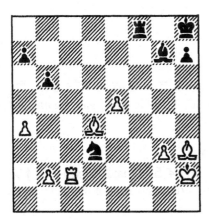

218. White to play (15 mins.)

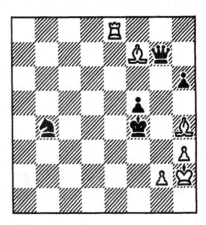

219. White to play (18 mins.)

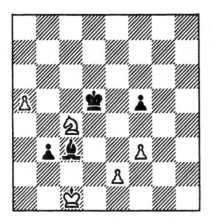

220. White to play (20 mins.)

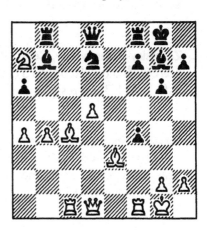

221. White to play (8 mins.)

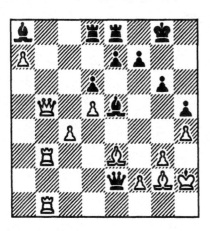

222. White to play (12 mins.)

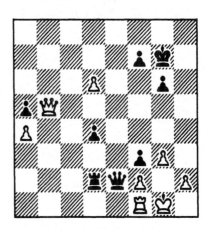

SOLUTIONS TO POSITIONS 217-222

217. Chekhlov-Batakov, Riga, 1974
1 e6! ♖e8 (on *1...♗xd4* White wins by *2 e7* and *3 ♖c8*) 2 e7! ♞c5 3 ♖f2! ♔g8 4 ♗xc5 bxc5 5 ♗e6+ ♔h8 6 ♖f7! Black resigns. There is no defence against 7 ♗d7.

218. Padevsky-Marjanovic, Vrnjacka Banja, 1973
1 g3+ ♔f3 2 ♗h5+ ♔f2 3 g4+ ♔f3 (not *3...♔f1 4 ♖e1* mate) 4 gxf5+ ♔f4 5 f6! Black resigns. There is no defence against the further advance of the pawn to f8.

219. Petrosian-Pomar, Havana, 1966
1 a6! ♔c6 2 ♞d6! ♗d4 (or *2...♔b6 3 a7 ♔xa7 4 ♞b5+*) 3 ♞xf5 ♗h8 4 e3 b2+ 5 ♔c2 ♔b6 6 ♞d4 ♔xa6 7 ♔xb2 Black resigns.

220. Zelinsky-Zhuravlyov, Corr., 1974
1 ♞c6! ♗xc6 2 dxc6 fxe3 3 c7!! ♕e7 4 ♖xf7!! ♖xf7 5 ♕xd7! ♕xd7 6 cxb8=♕+ ♗f8 7 ♖f1 Black resigns.

221. Bakulin-Shamkovich, Moscow, 1964 (variation)
1 ♕xe8+!! ♖xe8 2 ♖b8! ♖f8 3 ♖xf8+ ♔xf8 4 ♖b8+ ♔g7 5 ♖xa8, and White wins, since 5...♗xg3+ is met simply by 6 ♔xg3. In the game White missed this possibility, and played 1 f4?

222. Ermenkov-Sax, Warsaw, 1969
1 d7 d3 2 ♕b3 (Black was threatening *2...♕xf1+ 3 ♔xf1 ♖d1* mate) 2...♖c2 3 ♕a3 (defending against the same threat) 3...♕xf1+ (or *3...♖d2 4 ♕c3+* and *5 ♕xd2*) 4 ♔xf1 d2 5 ♕xf3 ♖c1+ 6 ♕d1!! Black resigns.

223. White to play (20 mins.)

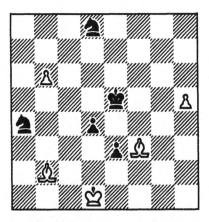

224. Black to play (10 mins.)

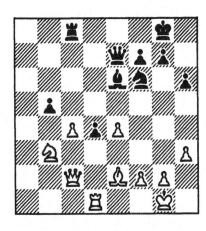

225. Black to play (14 mins.)

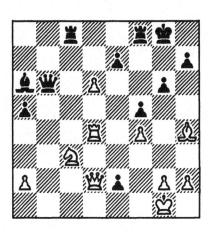

226. Black to play (20 mins.)

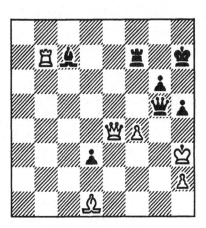

Theme: "Breakthrough" (Nos. 227-230)

227. Black to play (8 mins.)

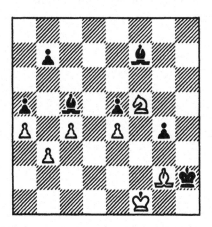

228. Black to play (10 mins.)

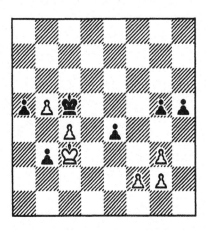

SOLUTIONS TO POSITIONS 223-228

223. Korchnoi-Parma, Yerevan, 1971
1 ♗xd4+!! ♔xd4 2 h6 ♘b2+ (if *2... ♘xb6 3 ♗h5!*) 3 ♔e2 ♘d3 4 ♗h5!! ♘f4+ 5 ♔d1 ♔d3 (or *5... ♘xh5 6 h7 ♘f7 7 b7!*) 6 h7! ♘f7 7 b7! Black resigns.

224. Bonasitz-Ortega, Havana, 1966
1...d3!! 2 ♖xd3 (if *2 ♗xd3 bxc4*, and Black wins a piece) 2...bxc4 3 ♖c3 cxb3! 4 ♖xc8+ ♗xc8 5 ♕xc8+ ♕e8 6 ♕xe8+ (on any other move Black plays *6...♕xe4*, with a won ending) 6...♘xe8 7 ♔f1 b2 8 ♗d3 ♘d6 9 ♔e1 ♘c4! White resigns.

225. Sokolov-Ni, Kishinyov, 1961
1...♖xc3!! 2 ♕xc3 ♖c8 3 dxe7 ♕xd4+!! 4 ♕xd4 ♖c1+ 5 ♗e1 ♖xe1+ 6 ♔f2 ♖f1+ 7 ♔g3 e1=Q+ 8 ♔h3 ♖f3+!! 9 g3 ♖xg3+! White resigns.

226. Gereben-Honfi, Bad Mondorf, 1974
1...♖xf4!! 2 ♖xc7+ ♔h6 3 ♕e1 d2! 4 ♕g3 ♕f5+ 5 ♔g2 ♕e4+ 6 ♔h3 (if *6 ♔g1* *♕e1+ 7 ♔g2 ♕f1 mate*) 6...h4! 7 ♕c3 ♕f5+ 8 ♔g2 ♖g4+ 9 ♗xg4 ♕xg4+ 10 ♔f2 d1=♘+! White resigns.

227. Paoli-Ciocaltea, Dortmund, 1973
1...b5!! 2 ♘h6 (if *2 axb5 ♗xc4+ 3 bxc4 a4!!*) 2...bxa4! 3 bxa4 ♗xc4+ 4 ♔e1 ♔xg2 5 ♘xg4 ♗d4 White resigns.

228. Kuznetsov-Selenskikh, Chelyabinsk, 1971
1...g4! 2 ♔xb3 h4! 3 gxh4 g3 4 fxg3 e3 5 ♔c2 e2 6 ♔d2 a4 White resigns.

229. White to play (5 mins.)

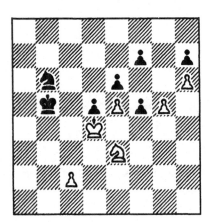

230. White to play (12 mins.)

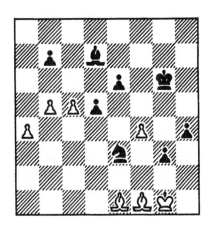

Theme: "Simplifying combinations" (Nos. 231-240)

231. Black to play (6 mins.)

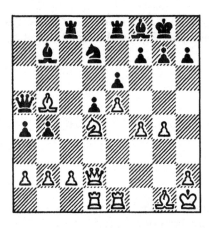

232. White to play (10 mins.)

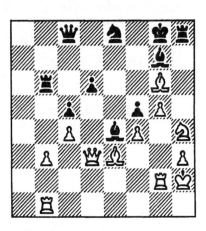

233. White to play (12 mins.)

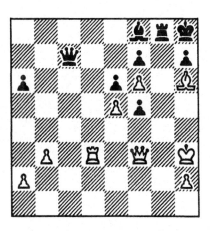

234. White to play (15 mins.)

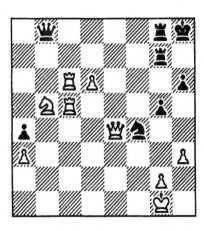

SOLUTIONS TO POSITIONS 229-234

229. Salo-Kupper, Amsterdam, 1954

1 ♘xf5!! exf5 2 e6! fxe6 3 g6! e5+ 4 ♔d3 hxg6 5 h7 ♔c5 6 h8=♕ Black resigns.

230. Lundin-Steiner, Vienna, 1951 (variation)

1 a5! ♘xf1 2 a6 bxa6 3 c6 ♗e8 (or *3...♗c8 4 b6*, and wins) 4 c7 ♗d7 5 bxa6 ♗c8 6 a7, and White wins.

231. Barden-Korchnoi, Leipzig, 1960

1...♕xb5!! 2 ♘xb5 d4+ 3 ♕g2 ♗xg2+ 4 ♔xg2 ♖xc2+ 5 ♔f3 ♖xb2 White resigns.

232. Stepak-Wolfiner, Tel Aviv, 1962

1 ♕xe4!! fxe4 2 ♗f5! ♖xh4 (no better is *2...♕d8 3 ♗e6+ ♔h7* - or *3...♔f8 4 ♘g6 mate - 4 g6+ ♔h6 5 ♘f5+ ♔h5 6 ♖bg1 ♗f6 7 g7*, and wins) 3 ♗xc8 ♗d4 4 ♗xd4 cxd4 5 ♔g3 Black resigns.

233. Kupper-Schmid, Zurich, 1956

1 ♗xf8! ♖xf8 2 ♕g2! ♖g8 3 ♖g3 ♕b8 4 ♖xg8+ ♕xg8 5 b4! ♕f8 6 ♕g7+! Black resigns (after *6...♕xg7 7 fxg7+ ♔xg7 8 a4* one of the white pawns queens).

234. Hajtun-Ciric, Budapest, 1957

1 d7 ♘g6 2 ♖xg6! ♖xg6 3 ♕xg6! ♖xg6 4 ♖c8+ ♖g8 5 ♖xb8 ♖xb8 6 ♘d6! ♔g7 (*6...♖d8 7 ♘f7+*) 7 ♘b7! Black resigns (but not *7 ♘c8 ♖b1+ and 8...♖d1*).

235. White to play (6 mins.)

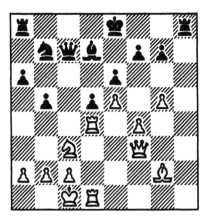

236. Black to play (12 mins.)

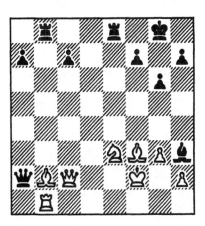

237. Black to play (12 mins.)

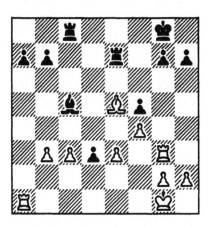

238. Black to play (15 mins.)

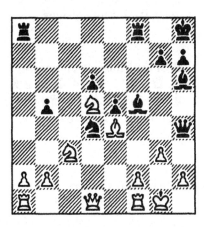

239. Black to play (18 mins.)

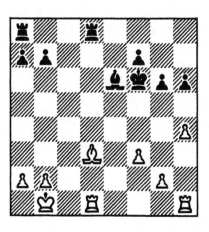

240. Black to play (15 mins.)

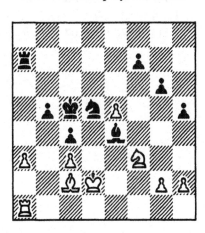

SOLUTIONS TO POSITIONS 235-240

235. Radulov-Hassani, Skopje, 1972

1 ♘xd5!! exd5 (or *1... ♛a5 2 ♘c7+!!*) 2 ♕xd5 0-0-0 3 ♕xb7+ ♕xb7 4 ♗xb7+ ♔xb7 5 ♖xd7+ ♔c8 6 ♖xf7 Black resigns.

236. Quinteros-Portisch, Manila, 1974

1... ♖xe3!! 2 ♘xe3 ♗f5 3 ♗e4 ♕b3+ 4 ♕xb3 ♖xb3+ 5 ♔f4 ♗xe4 6 ♔xe4 a5! 7 h4 h5 8 ♔f4 (no better is *8 ♔d4 a4*, when White ends up in zugzwang) 8...a4, and Black won.

237. Bobrov-Yusupov, Moscow, 1974

1... ♖xe5!! 2 fxe5 f4 3 ♖f3 ♗xe3+ 4 ♔f1 ♖xc3 5 g3 g5 6 gxf4 gxf4 7 b4 ♔f7 8 ♖h3 ♖c2 White resigns.

238. Bitman-Moiseyev, Moscow, 1972

1...♕xe4!! 2 ♘xe4 ♗xe4 3 ♘c3 (forced, in view of the threat of *3... ♗f3* and *4... ♘e2+*) 3...♗f3 4 ♕d3 b4 (Black wins a third piece for the queen, and his attack continues) 5 ♖fe1 bxc3 6 bxc3 ♖a3 7 ♖ab1 ♗a8 8 ♔f1 ♖xa2 9 f4 ♗g2+ White resigns.

239. Gheorghiu-Gligoric, Hastings, 1964/65

1... ♖xd3! 2 ♖xd3 ♗f5 3 ♖hd1 ♖d8 4 ♔c2 g5! 5 hxg5+ ♔xg5 6 g3 h5 7 ♔c3 ♖xd3+ 8 ♖xd3 ♗xd3 9 ♔xd3 f5 10 ♔e3 f4+ 11 ♔f2 b5! White resigns.

240. Dvoryetsky-Klovan, Tbilisi, 1973

1... ♘xc3!! 2 ♔xc3 ♖xa3+!! 3 ♖xa3 b4+ 4 ♔b2 bxa3+ 5 ♔xa3 ♗xc2 6 ♘g5 ♗b3 7 ♘xf7 ♔d5 8 ♔b4 ♔e6 9 ♘d6 ♔xe5 10 ♘xc4+ ♗xc4 White resigns.

Theme: "Drawing combinations" (Nos. 241-252)

241. Black to play and draw (6 mins.)

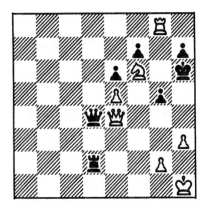

242. Black to play and draw (5 mins.)

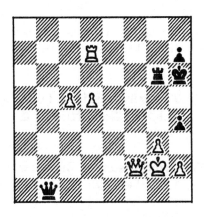

243. Black to play and draw (6 mins.)

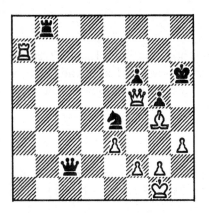

244. White to play (15 mins.)
Can he save the game?

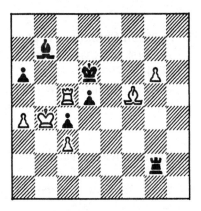

245. Black to play and draw (15 mins.)

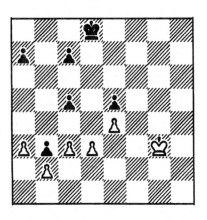

246. Black to play and draw (7 mins.)

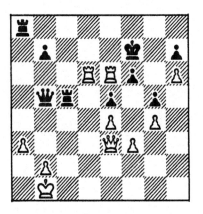

SOLUTIONS TO POSITIONS 241-246

241. Gogolev-Varshavsky, Aluksne, 1967
1...♖d1+! 2 ♔h2 ♕g1+! 3 ♔g3 ♖d3+! 4 ♕xd3 ♕e3+! 5 ♕xe3 - stalemate.

242. Tiberger-Dreskievic, Lodz, 1970
1...h3+! 2 ♔xh3 ♕f5+! 3 ♕xf5 ♖xg3+! 4 ♔h4 ♖g4+ 5 ♔xg4 - stalemate.

243. Ormos-Betotsky, Budapest, 1951
1...♖b1+! 2 ♔h2 ♖h1+! 3 ♔xh1 ♘g3+! 4 fxg3 ♕xg2+! 5 ♔xg2 - stalemate.

244. Kovacs-Portisch, Budapest, 1963
1 ♗c8!! ♖b2+ 2 ♔a5! ♔xc5 3 g7! ♖g2 4 ♗g4!! ♖xg4 5 g8=♕ ♖xg8 - stalemate.

245. Lukanin-Shmulian, Taganrog, 1948
The first impression is that Black's position is hopeless, but... 1...c4!! 2 dxc4 c5 3
♔g4 ♔c7! 4 ♔f5 ♔b6 5 ♔xe5 ♔a5 6 ♔d5 ♔a4 7 ♔xc5 a5!!, and Black is
stalemated whatever White plays. There is no way by which Black could have been
prevented from carrying out this idea.

246. Kopriva-Kabes, Novi Vcelnik, 1956
1...♕f1+ 2 ♔a2 ♖xa3+!! 3 ♔xa3 (if *3 bxa3 ♖c2+*, and it is Black who wins, or *3
♕xa3 ♕c4+* with perpetual check) 3...♕a1+ 4 ♔b4 (if *4 ♔b3 ♖b5+*) 4...♕a5+ 5
♔b3 ♕b5+ - draw.

247. Black to play and draw (5 mins.)

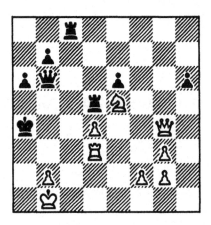

248. Black to play and draw (6 mins.)

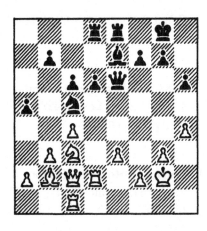

250. White to play (5 mins.)
How should White continue? What result can Black hope for?

249. Black to play and draw (8 mins.)

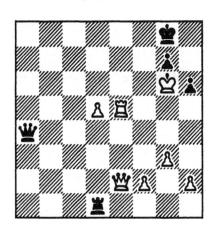

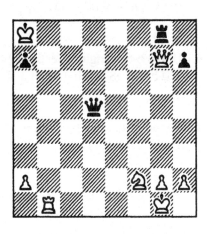

251. Black to play (6 mins.)
After 1...d3 can White save the game?

252. White to play (10 mins.)
How does White get out of his difficulties?

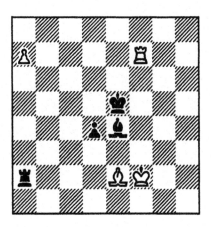

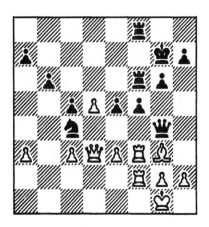

SOLUTIONS TO POSITIONS 247-252

247. Navai Ali-Shaligram, Bombay, 1959
1...♕xb2+!! 2 ♔xb2 ♖b5+ 3 ♔a2 ♖c2+ 4 ♔a1 ♖c1+ 5 ♔a2 ♖c2+, with a draw by perpetual check.

248. Petrosian-Rossetto, Buenos Aires, 1964
1...♗xh4! 2 gxh4 ♕g4+ 3 ♔f1 ♕h3+ 4 ♔e1 ♖xe3+! 5 fxe3 (*5 ♖e2* is bad because of *5... ♘d3+!*) 5...♕h1+ 6 ♔f2 ♕h2+ - draw.

249. Litkevic-Badenstein, Citau, 1957
1...♖e1!! 2 ♕f3! (or *2 ♕xe1 ♕g4+!*) 2...♕a6+ 3 ♖e6 ♖xe6+ 4 dxe6 ♕xe6+ 5 ♔h5 ♕h3+, with a draw by perpetual check.

250. Uhlrich-Sprengler, Berlin, 1948
1 ♖b5! ♖e8 2 ♖b1! ♖g8 3 ♖b5! - draw: both players are forced to repeat moves.

251. Barnes-Thompson, Manchester, 1946
1...d3 2 ♖e7+ ♔d4 3 ♖xe4+! ♔xe4 4 a8=Q+ ♖xa8 5 ♗f3+ - draw.

252. Zaitsev,A-Lutikov, Perm, 1971
1 ♗f4!! exf4 2 exf4 ♘a5 3 ♖g3 c4 4 ♕f1 ♕h4 5 ♖h3 ♕g4 6 ♖g3 - draw.

Theme: "Traps" (Nos. 253-268)

253. White to play (6 mins.)
White played 1 ♗d3, when it appears that Black can reply 1... ♖exb6. What is this, an oversight or a trap?

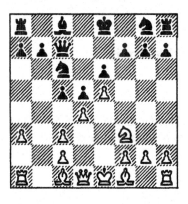

254. Black to play (7 mins.)
The impression is that after 1... ♞c7 Black should win, but is this so?

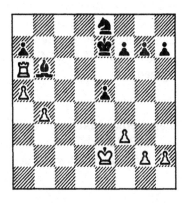

255. White to play (8 mins.)
After 1 ♗d3 can Black win a pawn by 1...cxd4 2 cxd4 ♞xd4?

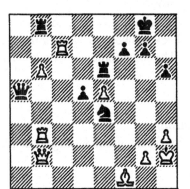

256. Black to play (7 mins.)
White was hoping for 1...♗xf4, on which he had prepared a counter-blow. What was it?

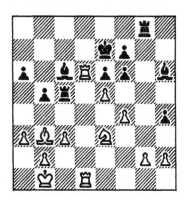

257. Black to play (8 mins.)
It appears that Black can capture the d4 pawn quite safely. But is this so? What did White have in mind?

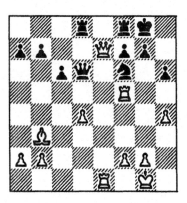

258. White to play (10 mins.)
White went 1 ♔f2!? What was he hoping for, since after 1... ♖g1 it is not apparent that he can avoid mate?

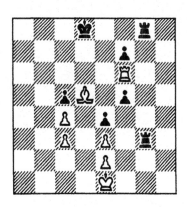

SOLUTIONS TO POSITIONS 253-258

253. Tukmakov-Bronstein, Moscow, 1972 (variation)
1 ♗d3! ♖exb6? 2 ♖xb6 ♖xb6 (or *2...♕xb6 3 ♖c8+!!*) 3 ♕f2!, and Black has no satisfactory way of defending f7. In the game Black answered 1 ♗d3 with 1...♖g6 2 ♗xe4 dxe4 3 ♕d4 e3 4 ♖xe3 ♕xb6 5 ♕xb6 ♖bxb6, whereupon a draw was agreed.

254. Panchenko-Marjanovic, Tbilisi, 1973 (variation)
1...♘c7?? 2 axb6!! ♘xa6 3 b5!!, and White wins. In the game 1...♗g1 was played, and the final result was a draw.

255. Booth-Fazekas, London, 1946
1 ♗d3 cxd4 2 cxd4 ♘xd4? 3 ♘xd4 ♕c3+ 4 ♕d2!! ♕xa1 5 c3!, and Black cannot avoid the loss of his queen after 6 ♘b3.

256. Gligoric-Nievergelt, Zurich, 1959
1...♗xf4? 2 ♘f5+! exf5 3 exf6+ ♔f8 4 ♖xc6! Black resigns.

257. Pasman-Saigin, Riga, 1961
1...♕xd4? 2 ♖d1 ♕e4 3 ♗xf7+! ♔h7 (or *3...♔h8 4 ♕xd8 ♖xd8 5 ♖xd8+ ♔h7 6 h5!*, and wins) 4 ♗g6+!! Black resigns (*4...♔xg6 5 ♖xf6+*, or *4...♔g8 5 ♕xd8*).

258. Perez-Ivkov, Havana, 1962
1 ♔f2!? ♖g1? 2 ♗xe4 fxe4 3 ♖d6+! ♔e7 4 ♖e6+! - draw. After 4...♔f8 5 ♖e8+ ♔g7 6 ♖xg8+ ♔xg8 7 ♔xg1 White cannot lose.

259. Black to play (8 mins.)
Black played 1...♕xc3. What was the cunning trap that he had overlooked?

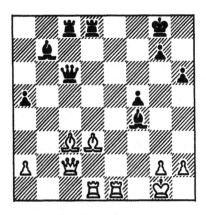

260. Black to play (6 mins.)
Black decided that he could safely capture the d5 pawn by 1...Nxd5, but is this so?

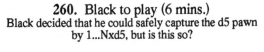
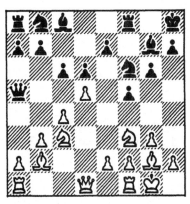

261. White to play (7 mins.)
White realized that, with normal play, Black would win sooner or later, and so he set a trap by 1 d6, hoping for 1... cxd6. What was the point? What should Black play?

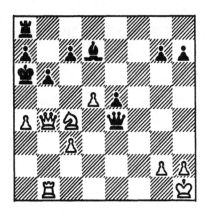

262. Black to play (5 mins.)
After 1..Be6 Black's position would be no worse. But he decided that after 1...0-0, 2 ♕xe7 would be bad on account of 2...♕d4+. Is this so?

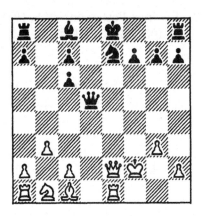

263. Black to play (7 mins.)
Black decided to play 1...♘xh2, and if 2 ♖h4 ♘xf3+, but he thereby fell into what well-concealed trap?

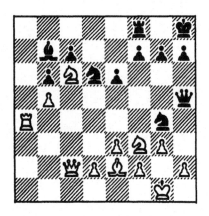

264. Black to play (10 mins.)
Neglecting the safety of his own king, Black threatened White's with 1...♘xf3?, and was immediately punished.

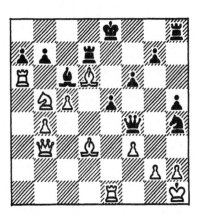

SOLUTIONS TO POSITIONS 259-264

259. **Dvoiris-Spassky, Moscow, 1974 (from a simultaneous display with clocks)**
   1...♛xc3? 2 ♗c4+!! ♖xc4 3 ♖xd8+ ♔f7 4 ♛xf5+ ♛f6 5 ♖e7+! Black resigns.

260. **Robatsch-Jansa, Sochi, 1974**
   1...♞xd5?? 2 cxd5! ♗xc3 3 ♛d2!! ♛xd5 4 ♛xc3+ e5 5 ♞xe5! Black resigns.

261. **Bogatirev-Emelianov, Moscow, 1975**
   1 d6 cxd6?? (Black should have played *1...♗c6! 2 ♖g1 ♖f8!* - threatening
   3...♛xg2+!! - 3 h3 ♖f1!) 2 ♛b5+! ♗xb5 3 axb5+ ♔b7 4 ♞xd6+ ♔c7 5 ♞xe4
   Black resigns.

262. **Boatner-Patterson, USA, 1958**
   1...0-0?? 2 ♛xe7!! ♛d4+ 3 ♗e3 ♛xa1 4 ♛xf8+!! ♔xf8 5 ♗c5+ Black resigns.

263. **Bernstein-Seidman, New York, 1959**
   1...♞xh2?? 2 ♞fe5!! ♛xe2 3 ♛xh7+!! ♔xh7 4 ♖h4+ ♔g8 5 ♞e7 mate.

264. **Mileika-Verk, Riga, 1960**
   1...♞xf3?? 2 ♞c7+! ♖xc7 3 ♛e6+ ♔d8 4 ♗xc7+ ♔xc7 5 ♛d6+ ♔c8 6 ♖xc6+!!
   bxc6 7 ♗a6 mate.

265. White to play (10 mins.)
Black appears to have overlooked 1 ♘d5, winning the exchange. But is this so?

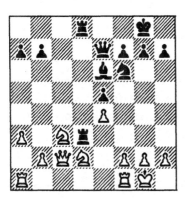

266. Black to play (7 mins.)
Black chose the forcing continuation 1...♖a1+ 2 ♔f2 ♖f1+, thinking that this would win. But does it?

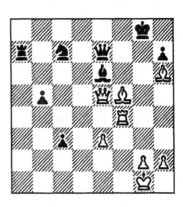

267. White to play (8 mins.)
It appears very tempting for White to capture the undefended rook at f8. But what is the price he has to pay?

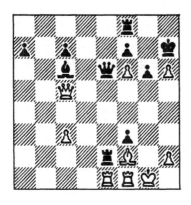

268. Black to play (7 mins.)
White's last move, 1 ♗d4, looks like an oversight. It appears that by 1...♗c5 Black can get out of the unpleasant pin, but is this so?

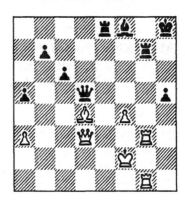

Theme: "Attack on the kingside castled position" (Nos. 269-288)

269. White to play (12 mins.)

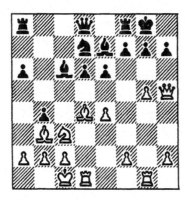

270. White to play (15 mins.)

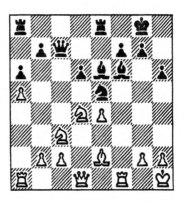

SOLUTIONS TO POSITIONS 265-270

265. **Zabaleta-de Visente, Madrid, 1958**
1 ♘d5?? ♘xd5!! 2 ♕xd3 ♘f4!! 3 ♕e2 ♖xd2!! (other queen moves would have been answered in the same way) 4 ♕xd2 ♕g5! 5 ♕xf4 (forced, since Black was threatening both mate at g2, and *5... ♘h3+*) 5...exf4, and Black won.

266. **Boze-Denik, Corr., 1963**
1... ♖a1+ 2 ♔f2 ♖f1+? 3 ♔xf1 ♗c4+ 4 ♗d3 ♗xd3+ 5 ♔f2 ♕xe5 6 ♖f8 mate.

267. **Schwankrais-Aisinger, Karlsruhe, 1964**
1 ♕xf8?? ♕g4+ 2 ♗g3 ♖g2+ 3 ♔h1 ♖xh2+! 4 ♔xh2 ♕h5+ 5 ♔g1 f2+! 6 ♔xf2 ♕f3+ 7 ♔g1 ♕g2 mate.

268. **Mista-Kloza, Poland, 1955**
1...♗c5?? 2 ♕xh7+!! ♔xh7 3 ♖xg7+ ♔h8 4 ♖g8+ ♔h7 5 ♖1g7+ ♔h6 6 ♖g6+ ♔h7 7 ♖8g7+ ♔h8 8 ♖h6 mate.

269. **Steczkowski-Grulka, Lublin, 1969**
1 ♖d3!! bxc3 (*1...g6* fails to *2 ♕xh7+*, while on the comparatively best *1... ♖e8, 2 g6!!* decides) 2 ♖h3 ♗xe4 3 g6!! h6 (if *3...♗xg6 4 ♕xh7+! ♗xh7 5 ♖xg7+* and *6 ♖hxh7* mate) 4 gxf7+ ♖xf7 5 ♕xh6 Black resigns.

270. **Karasev-Ioffe, Leningrad, 1969**
1 ♖xf6!! gxf6 2 ♕d2 ♘c6 3 ♘f5! ♗xf5 4 ♘d5! ♕d8 5 ♕xh6 ♗g6 6 ♖a3 Black resigns.

271. Black to play (16 mins.)

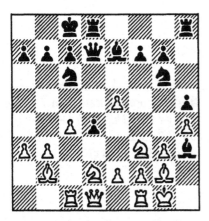

272. White to play (20 mins.)

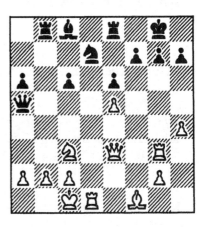

273. White to play (15 mins.)

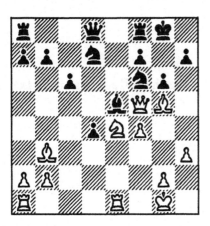

274. White to play (20 mins.)

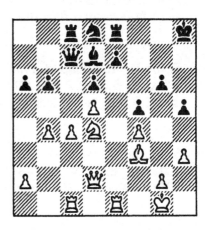

275. White to play (12 mins.)

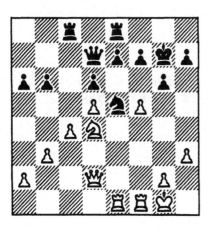

276. White to play (12 mins.)

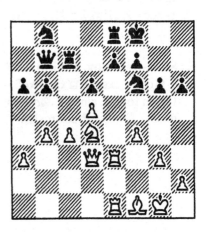

SOLUTIONS TO POSITIONS 271-276

271. Shapiro-Kneller, Liepaja, 1972
1...♗xh4!! 2 ♗xh3 (White loses immediately after *2 gxh4 ♕g4 or 2 ♘xh4 ♘xh4 3 gxh4 ♕g4*) 2...♕xh3 3 ♘xh4 ♘xh4 4 gxh4 ♕g4+ (more accurate than *4... ♖h6 5 ♘f3 ♖g6+ 6 ♘g5 f6 7 exf6 gxf6 8 ♕d3, or 6... ♕g4+ 7 ♔h2 ♕xh4+ 8 ♘h3*) 5 ♔h1 ♕xh4+ 6 ♔g2 ♖h6 7 ♕c2 (or *7 f4 ♖g6+ 8 ♘f3 ♕g3+ 9 ♔e4 ♕e3+ 10 ♔f5 ♘e7 mate*) 7...♕g4+ 8 ♔h2 d3! White resigns (*9 exd3 ♖g6!*).

272. Keres-Szabo, Budapest, 1955
1 ♖xd7!! ♗xd7 2 ♗d3!! h6 (*2...g6 is not good in view of 3 h5, while in the event of 2... ♖xb2 3 ♔xb2 ♖b8+ 4 ♔c1 Black has nothing for the sacrificed material*) 3 ♕f4! ♔f8 (the threat was *4 ♕f6*) 4 ♖xg7! ♔xg7 5 ♕f6+ ♔f8 (or *5... ♔g8 6 ♕xh6*, with the threat of *7 ♗h7+, 8 ♗g6+ and 9 ♕h7+*, while *6... ♖e7 fails to 7 ♕h7+ and 8 ♕h8 mate*) 6 ♗g6 Black resigns.

273. Szabo-Honfi, Budapest, 1950
1 ♕xe5!! ♘xe5 2 ♘xf6+ ♔h8 3 fxe5 ♕c7 4 ♖e4 h5 5 ♖ae1 ♔g7 6 e6! fxe6 7 ♖xe6 ♖f7 8 ♘e8+ Black resigns.

274. Szabo-Bertok, Vinkovci, 1970
1 ♗xh5! gxh5 2 ♕e2 ♘f7 3 ♕xh5+ ♔g7 4 ♖c3 ♖h8 5 ♖g3+ ♔f8 6 ♕g6! ♕xc4 7 ♕g7+ ♔e8 8 ♕g8+ ♖xg8 9 ♖xg8 mate.

275. Pipitone-Rossi, Italy, 1968
1 ♖xe5!! dxe5 2 ♘e6+!! ♔h8 (or *2...fxe6 3 fxe6 ♕c7 4 ♖f7+ ♔h8 5 ♕h6!*) 3 ♕h6 ♖g8 4 ♘g5 ♖g7 5 fxg6 f6 (if *5...fxg6 6 ♘e6 ♖cg8 7 ♘xg7 - not 7 ♖f8 ♕xe6 - 7... ♖xg7 8 ♖f8+ ♖g8 9 ♖f7*) 6 ♘xh7 ♔g8 7 ♖xf6 Black resigns.

276. Stein-Daskalov, Tallinn, 1971
1 ♘e6+!! fxe6 2 ♕xg6 exd5 (there is no other defence against *3 dxe6*) 3 ♗h3 e5 (again forced, since *4 ♗e6* was threatened) 4 ♕xf6+ ♖f7 5 ♕h8+ ♔e7 6 ♖xe5+ dxe5 7 ♕xe5+ Black resigns.

277. White to play (18 mins.)

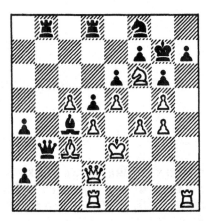

278. Black to play (20 mins.)

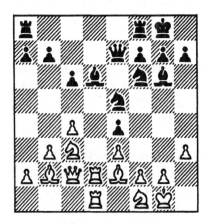

279. White to play (12 mins.)

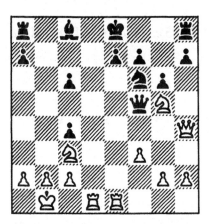

280. White to play (16 mins.)

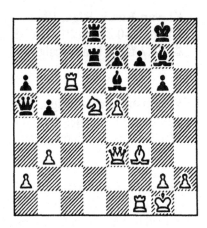

281. White to play (20 mins.)

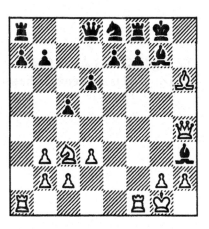

282. White to play (12 mins.)

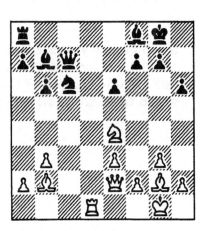

SOLUTIONS TO POSITIONS 277-282

277. Smyslov-Rubinetti, Palma de Mallorca, 1970
1 f5! exf5 2 gxf5 ♕a3 3 ♔f4! gxf5 4 ♖xh7+!! ♘xh7 5 ♕h2 ♘xg5 6 ♕g3 ♔f8 7 ♕xg5 ♕xc3 8 e6! Black resigns.

278. Kaufman-Kavalek, USA, 1972
1...♘f3+! 2 gxf3 exf3 3 ♗d3 ♕e6! 4 ♘g3 (no better is *4 ♘h2*, when Black wins by either *4...♗xh2+ 5 ♔xh2 ♕e5+ 6 ♔h1 ♕h5 7 ♔h2 ♘g4+ 8 ♔g3 ♘e5! 9 ♔h2 ♗xd3 10 ♖xd3 ♕g6!*, or *4...♕xh3 5 ♘xf3 ♕g4+ 6 ♔f1 ♕xf3! 7 ♗xg6 fxg6 8 ♖xd6 ♘g4!*) 4...♕xh3 5 ♗f1 ♕h6! (if *5...♕h4 6 ♖d4!*) 6 ♗d3 ♘g4 7 ♘ce4 ♕h3! White resigns.

279. Klovan-Etruk, Riga, 1964
1 ♕xc4 0-0 2 ♘xf7!! ♖xf7 3 ♖xe7 ♘d5 4 ♘xd5 cxd5 5 ♖e8+ ♖f8 6 ♖xf8+ ♔xf8 7 ♕c6! Black resigns.

280. Vitolinsh-Telman, Riga, 1967
1 ♖xe6!! fxe6 2 ♗g4! ♖xd5 3 ♗xe6+ ♔h7 4 ♕h3+ ♗h6 5 ♖f7+ ♔g8 6 ♖xe7+ ♔f8 7 ♕f3+ Black resigns.

281. Balashov-Tseitlin, Barnaul, 1969
1 ♘e4! (Black thought that White was bound to recapture on h3; after the move played he has no time to retreat his bishop, since after *2 ♘g5*, mate is inevitable) 1...♕d7 2 ♗xg7 ♘xg7 3 gxh3 f6 (if *3...♘e6, 4 ♖f2* is decisive) 4 ♖ae1 ♖f7 5 ♖c2! ♖af8 6 ♖g2 d5 7 ♖g6! (now there is no adequate defence against *8 ♖h6*) 7...dxe4 8 ♖h6 Black resigns.

282. Szabo-Padevsky, Amsterdam, 1972
1 ♘f6+! gxf6 (or *1...♔h8 2 ♖d7 and 3 ♖xf7*) 2 ♕g4+ ♔h7 3 ♗e4+ f5 4 ♗xf5+ exf5 5 ♕xf5+ ♔g8 6 ♖d7 ♕xd7 7 ♕xd7 ♖b8 (*7...♘d8* is answered in the same way) 8 ♕g4+ ♔h7 9 ♕f5+ Black resigns.

283. White to play (20 mins.)

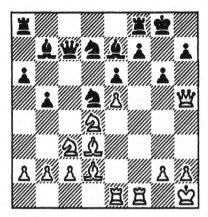

284. Black to play (20 mins.)

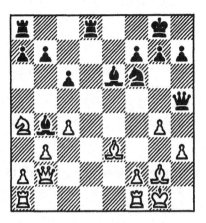

285. White to play (10 mins.)

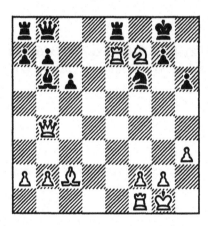

286. White to play (15 mins.)

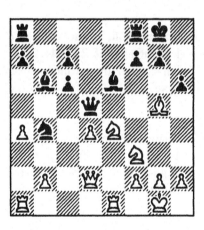

287. Black to play (20 mins.)

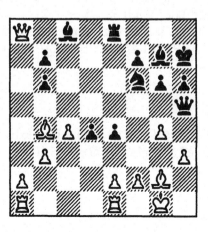

288. White to play (20 mins.)

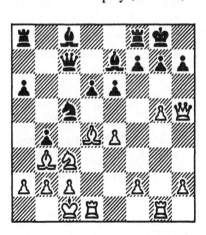

SOLUTIONS TO POSITIONS 283-288

283. Malevsky-Peshina, Kaliningrad, 1969

1 ♘xe6!! gxh5 (or *1...fxe6 2 ♗xg6! hxg6 3 ♕xg6+*) 2 ♘xd5 ♕b8 3 ♘xe7+ ♔h8 4 ♘xf8 ♖xf8 5 e6! ♕g7 6 ♖f2 fxe6 7 ♖xe6 ♕xb2 (there is no other defence against *8 ♗c3*) 8 ♖f7 ♘f8 9 ♖ef6 ♘g6 10 ♗xg6 Black resigns.

284. Palatnik-Bronstein, Tbilisi, 1973

1...♗xg4! 2 hxg4 ♘xg4 3 ♗f4 ♗d6! (less convincing is *3... ♖d2 4 ♕c1*, with possibilities of a defence) 4 ♗xd6 (on *4 ♕d2* there follows *4...♕h2+! 5 ♗xh2 ♗xh2+ 6 ♔h1 ♖xd2*, and Black wins) 4...♖xd6 5 ♖fe1 ♖g6! 6 ♘c3 (if *6 ♕e2 ♕h2+! 7 ♔f1 ♕h1+!! 8 ♘xh1 ♘h2 mate*) 6...♕h2+ 7 ♔f1 ♘f6! 8 ♘e4 ♕h3+ 9 ♔e2 ♘xe4 10 ♘xe4 ♖e6 White resigns.

285. Szabo-Paoli, Trencianskie Teplice, 1949

1 ♘xh6+! gxh6 2 ♕c4+ ♔h8 (or *2... ♘d5 3 ♕g4+*) 3 ♕f7 ♖xe7 4 ♕xf6+! ♔g8 (on *4... ♖g7* there follows *5 ♕xh6+ ♔g8 6 ♗b3+ ♔f8 7 ♕h8+*) 5 ♗b3+ ♔h7 6 ♕xe7+ ♔h8 7 ♕f6+ ♔h7 8 ♗c2+ Black resigns.

286. Nezhmetdinov-Golenishev, Archangelsk, 1963

1 ♗xh6! a5 2 ♘f6+!! gxf6 3 ♖e5!! ♕d7 (*3...fxe5 4 ♕g5+* and *5 ♕g7 mate*) 4 ♖g5+! ♔h7 5 ♖g7+ ♔h8 6 ♖g3 ♗g4 7 ♗xf8 ♖xf8 8 ♕h6+ ♔g8 9 h3 Black resigns.

287. Gergeli-Civic, Corr., 1972/73

1...♗xg4!! 2 hxg4 ♘xg4 3 ♕xb7 (White loses after *3 ♕xe8 ♕h2+ 4 ♔f1 ♕f4!!*, and now *5 f3 ♘e3+ 6 ♔f2 ♕h4+ 7 ♔g1 ♕g3* and *8...♕xg2 mate*, or *5 ♗f3 exf3 6 ♖eb1 - 6 exf3 ♕xf3 - 6...fxe2+ 7 ♕xe2 d3! 8 ♕d2 ♕h2*) 3...♕h2+ 4 ♔f1 e3! 5 fxe3 (the threat was *5...exf2 and 6...♕g1 mate*) 5...♕g3 6 ♔g1 (no better is *6 ♕f3 ♘h2+*) 6...♕xe3+ 7 ♔h1 ♘f2+ 8 ♔g1 ♘h3+ 9 ♔h1 ♕g1+!! 10 ♖xg1 ♘f2+ 11 ♔h2 ♗e5 mate.

288. Hennings-Mohring, East Germany, 1967

1 ♗f6!! ♖e8 (*1...bxc3 is bad on account of 2 ♕h6!!*) 2 ♖g3 bxc3 3 ♖h3 cxb2+ 4 ♔b1 ♗xf6 5 gxf6 ♔f8 6 e5 ♘e4 7 fxg7+ ♔e7 8 ♕h4+ f6 9 ♕xe4 d5 10 g8=♕ ♖xg8 11 ♕xh7+ Black resigns.

Theme: "Attack on the king caught in the centre" (Nos. 289-308)

289. White to play (20 mins.)

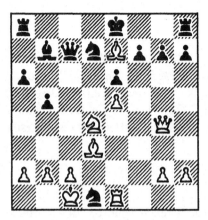

290. White to play (8 mins.)

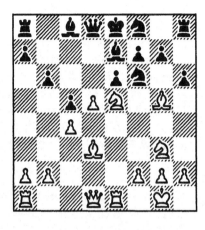

291. White to play (5 mins.)

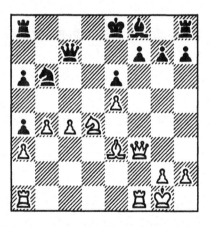

292. White to play (12 mins.)

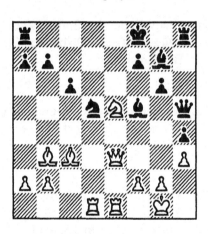

293. White to play (10 mins.)

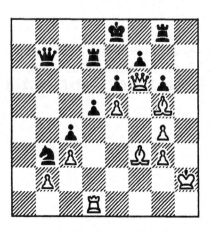

294. Black to play (15 mins.)

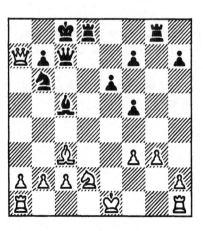

SOLUTIONS TO POSITIONS 289-294

289. Spassky-Rashkovsky, Moscow, 1973

1 ♘xe6!! ♕c6 (*1...fxe6 loses to 2 ♗d6! ♕b6 3 ♕g5! ♔f7 4 ♕e7+ ♔g8 5 ♕xe6 mate, or 3...♕d8 4 ♕g6+!!*) 2 ♘xg7+!! ♔xe7 3 ♕g5+ f6 (on *3...♔f8 there follows 4 ♘f5! ♕g6 5 ♕e7+ ♔g8 6 ♕xd7 ♕g5+ 7 ♔xd1 ♗xg2 8 ♖e3*) 4 exf6+ ♔d8 5 f7+ ♔c7 (or *5...♕f6 6 ♗e6+ ♔e7 - 6...♔c8 7 ♕g8+! - 7 ♘c5+ ♔d8 8 ♘xb7+ ♔c7 9 ♕xf6 ♘xf6 10 ♖e7+ followed by 11 ♔xd1*) 6 ♕f4+ Black resigns (since if *6...♔c8 7 ♖e8+!, or 6...♔b6 7 ♖e6!*).

290. Shiyanovsky-Lipnitsky, Kiev, 1952

1 ♘f5! ♘g6 (if *1...exf5 2 ♗xf6, and there is no defence against 3 ♘c6, while if 1... ♖g8 2 ♘c6*) 2 ♘xg7+ ♔f8 3 ♗xf6 ♗xf6 4 ♘xe6+! Black resigns.

291. Kirov-Padevsky, Sofia, 1972

1 ♘xe6!! fxe6 2 ♗xb6 ♕xb6+ 3 c5 ♕a7 4 ♕c6+ ♔e7 5 ♕d6+ ♔e8 6 ♕xe6+ Black resigns.

292. Najdorf-Rossetto, Buenos Aires, 1973

1 ♖xd5! cxd5 2 ♘xf7!! ♗xc3 3 bxc3 ♖h7 4 ♕e7+ ♔g8 5 ♗xd5 ♖g7 6 ♕e8+!! Black resigns.

293. Lundin-Momo, Leipzig, 1960

1 ♗xd5!! exd5 (*1... ♖xd5 2 ♕d8+! ♖xd8 3 ♖xd8 mate, or 1...♕c7 2 ♗c6! ♕xc6 3 ♕d8+*) 2 e6 fxe6 3 ♕xe6+ ♔f8 4 ♗h6+ ♖gg7 5 ♖e1 ♖de7 (or *5...♕c8 6 ♖f1+*) 6 ♕f6+ ♔e8 (*6...♔g8 7 ♗xg7*) 7 ♕xg7 Black resigns.

294. Troianescu-Szabo, Bucharest, 1947

1... ♖xd2!! 2 ♗xd2 (*2 ♔xd2 fails to 2... ♘c4+*) 2...♕e5+ 3 ♔f1 (even worse is *3 ♔d1 ♖d8, with the threat of 4... ♖xd2+ and 5... ♘c4+, while 4 ♕a5 is met by 4... ♘c4*) 3...♕d4 4 ♗e1 ♕c4+ 5 ♔g2 ♕e2+ 6 ♔h3 ♖g6 7 g4 ♕xf3+ 8 ♗g3 ♖h6 mate.

295. White to play (10 mins.)

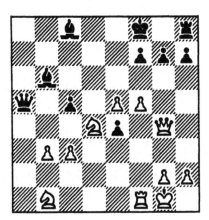

296. White to play (12 mins.)

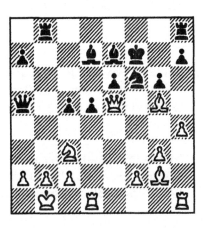

297. Black to play (7 mins.)

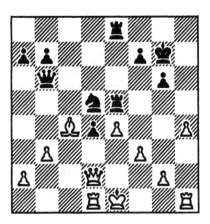

298. White to play (15 mins.)

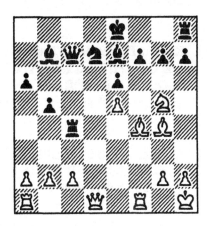

299. Black to play (12 mins.)

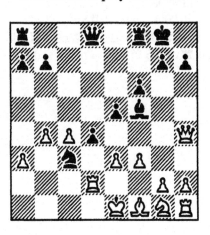

300. White to play (10 mins.)

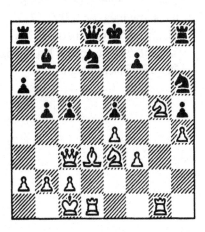

SOLUTIONS TO POSITIONS 295-300

295. **Zaitsev,I-Savon, Moscow, 1969**
1 ♘e6+! ♗xe6 (bad is *1...fxe6 2 fxe6+ ♔g8 3 e7!*) 2 fxe6 c4+ 3 ♔h1 ♕xe5 4 exf7 ♔e7 5 ♖f5 ♔e6 6 ♕xg7 Black resigns.

296. **Newspaper Readers-Krupsky, Gomel, 1970**
1 ♘xd5! exd5 2 ♗xd5+ ♘xd5 3 ♖xd5 ♗e6 4 ♕f4+ ♗f5 5 ♖xf5+! gxf5 6 ♕xf5+ ♔e8 7 ♕e5! Black resigns (*7...♔d7 8 ♖d1+ ♔c6 9 ♕e6+!*).

297. **Saveliev-Gerasimov, Moscow, 1970**
1...♖xe4+! 2 fxe4 ♖xe4+ 3 ♔f1 ♘e3+ 4 ♔g1 ♘xd1 5 ♕xd1 d3+ 6 ♔h2 ♕f2! 7 ♕xd3 ♖xh4+ White resigns.

298. **Klovan-Dementiev, Vilnius, 1972**
1 ♘xf7! ♔xf7 2 ♗xe6+! ♔xe6 3 ♕g4+ ♔f7 4 e6+ ♔g8 (*4...♔e8 5 ♕xg7!*) 5 exd7 ♕c6 6 ♖ae1 ♖e4 7 ♖xe4 ♕xe4 8 ♗d6!! Black resigns. There is no defence against 9 d8=♕+! ♗xd8 10 ♖f8 mate.

299. **Quinteros-Ribli, Montilla, 1974**
1...dxe3!! 2 ♖xd8 ♖axd8 3 ♗e2 ♖d2 (threatening *4...♗d3*, while if *4 ♔f1 ♗xe2*) 4 g4 ♗d3 5 ♔f1 ♘xe2 6 ♘xe2 ♖xe2 7 ♔g1 ♖d8 White resigns. After the bishop moves from d3 there is no defence against the mate.

300. **Kupreichik-Lutikov, Sochi, 1970**
1 ♗xb5! (the quickest and most effective winning path; also good was *1 ♗c4* with the same idea, or *1 ♗f1 ♕e7 2 ♘h3 0-0-0 3 ♘d5*) 1...axb5 2 ♖xd7! ♔xd7 (*2...♕xd7* is very bad in view of *3 ♕xe5+* and *4 ♕xh8*) 3 ♖d1+ ♔c6 4 ♖xd8 ♖hxd8 5 b4 f6 (*5...c4* brings no relief after *6 ♕xe5*) 6 ♕xc5+ ♔d7 7 ♘d5 ♗xd5 8 ♕xd5+ Black resigns.

301. White to play (8 mins.)

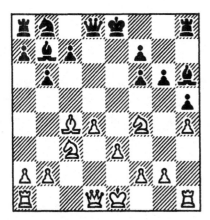

302. White to play (15 mins.)

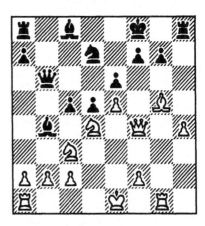

303. White to play (18 mins.)

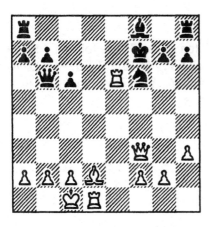

304. White to play (15 mins.)

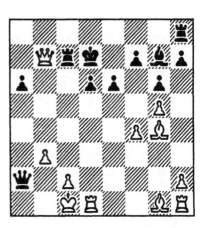

305. White to play (12 mins.)

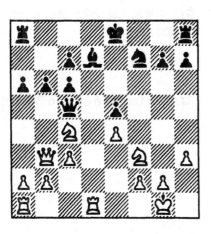

306. White to play (15 mins.)

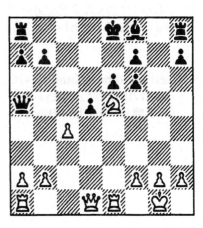

SOLUTIONS TO POSITIONS 301-306

301. Vaganian-Botterill, Hastings, 1974/75

1 ♗xf7+!! ♔xf7 2 ♕b3+ ♔e8 3 ♘xg6 (*3 ♕e6+ is weaker in view of 3...♕e7 4 ♕xe7+ ♔xe7 5 ♘xg6+ ♔f7 6 ♘xh8+ ♔g7*) 3...♕d7 4 ♘xh8 ♕g7 5 ♕e6+ ♔f8 6 ♘d5 ♘d7 7 ♘e7! Black resigns. The white knights are invulnerable, and there is no defence against 8 ♘eg6+.

302. Urzica-Ghinde, Bucharest, 1975

1 ♗d8! ♕a6 (*1...♕xd8 2 ♘xe6+*) 2 ♖xg7! ♔xg7 (if *2...♕xe5 3 ♕xe5 cxd4 4 ♕xd4 ♗e7 5 ♗xe7+ ♔xe7 6 0-0-0*) 3 ♕g5+ ♔f8 4 ♗e7+! ♔e8 5 ♗d6 ♘f6 (no better is *5...f6 6 ♕g6+ ♔d8 7 ♘xe6* mate) 6 ♕xf6 ♕b7 7 ♘c6 ♗xc3+ 8 bxc3 ♔d7 9 ♘a5! Black resigns.

303. Boleslavsky-Flohr, Moscow, 1950 (variation)

1 ♖xf6+!! gxf6 2 ♕h5+ ♔g8 3 ♕g4+ ♔f7 (on *3...♗g7 there follows 4 ♕e6+ ♔f8 5 ♗f4!*) 4 ♕c4+ ♔g6 (if *4...♔g7 5 ♗e3 ♕c7 6 ♕g4+ ♔f7 7 ♗d7+*) 5 ♕e4+ ♔f7 (or *5...♔g7 6 ♗e3 ♕c7 7 ♕g4+*) 6 ♗a5! ♕c5 (*6...♕xa5 loses to 7 ♖d7+*) 7 ♖d7+ ♗e7 8 ♗b4 ♕g5+ 9 f4, and White wins.

304. Krasilnikov-Bogoslovsky, Yaroslavl, 1951

1 ♖xd6+! ♔xd6 2 ♗c5+! ♖xc5 (or *2...♔xc5 3 ♕xc7+*) 3 ♖d1+ ♗d4 (if *3...♖d5 4 ♖xd5+ exd5 5 ♕b6+ ♔e7 6 ♕c7+ ♔e8 7 ♕d7+ ♔f8 8 ♕d8 mate*) 4 ♖xd4+ ♖d5 5 ♖xd5+ exd5 6 ♕d7+ ♔c5 7 ♕c7+ ♔d4 (or *7...♔b4 8 ♕b6+*) 8 ♔d2 Black resigns.

305. Mecking-Rocha, Mar del Plata, 1969

1 ♖xd7!! ♔xd7 2 ♘xb6+! ♕xb6 3 ♕xf7+ ♔c8 4 ♘xe5 ♕xb2 5 ♕d7+ ♔b8 6 ♕d1! ♕xc3 7 ♖b1+ ♔a7 8 ♕d4+! ♕xd4 9 ♘xc6 mate.

306. Nezhmetdinov-Kamishev, Gorky, 1950

1 ♘xf7!! ♔xf7 2 ♕h5+ ♔e7 3 cxd5 e5 4 f4 ♕xd5 5 fxe5 f5 6 e6 ♔f6 7 h4! ♗d6 8 ♔h1 ♕xe6 9 ♕h6+ Black resigns.

307. White to play (20 mins.)

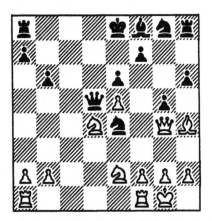

308. White to play (20 mins.)

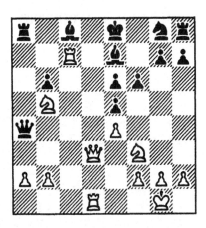

Theme: "Destructive combinations" (Nos. 309-378)

309. Black to play (8 mins.)

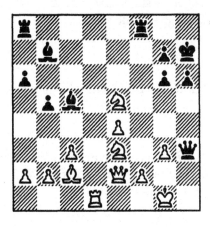

310. Black to play (6 mins.)

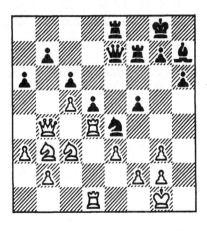

311. White to play (12 mins.)

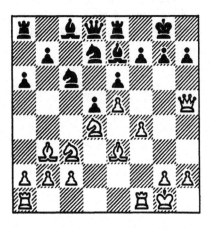

312. White to play (12 mins.)

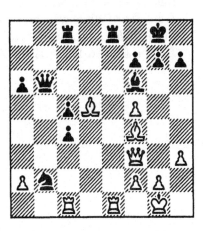

SOLUTIONS TO POSITIONS 307-312

307. Mista-Fichtl, Prague, 1974

1 ♘xe6! fxe6 2 ♕h5+ ♔e7 3 ♗f4!! ♕b5 (or *3...gxh4 4 ♘xd5+ exd5 5 ♖ac1*) 4 ♖ac1! ♖d8 (forced, in view of the threat of *5 ♖c7+ ♔d8 6 ♘xe6* mate) 5 ♘g6+ ♔f7 6 ♖c7+ ♖d7 7 ♖c8! ♘ef6 8 exf6 ♘xf6 9 ♘xh8+ Black resigns.

308. Tilet-Gakometti, Corr., 1956

1 b3! ♕b4! 2 a3! ♕a5 3 ♕d8+!! ♔f7 (*3...♗xd8 4 ♘d6+ and 5 ♖f7* mate) 4 ♘d6+ ♔g6 5 ♕e8+ ♔h6 6 ♘f7+ ♔h5 7 ♘7xe5+ g6 8 g4+ ♔h6 9 ♖xe7 ♗b7 (or *9... ♗xe7 10 ♕xh8*) 10 ♖xh7+ Black resigns (the next move is *11 ♕xg6* mate).

309. Gurgenidze-Nezhmetdinov, Tbilisi, 1957

1...♖xf2!! 2 ♔xf2 (or *2 ♕xf2 ♖f8! 3 ♕e1 ♖f1+! 4 ♕xf1 ♗xe3+ 5 ♕f2 ♕xg3+*) 2...♕h2+ 3 ♔e1 ♕xg3+ 4 ♔d2 ♕xe5 5 ♘d5 ♕g5+ White resigns.

310. Sazhayev-Mokin, Chelyabinsk, 1973

1...♘xf2!! 2 ♔xf2 ♕xe3+ 3 ♔f1 f4! 4 gxf4 ♖xf4+ 5 ♖xf4 ♗d3+! White resigns.

311. Troinov-Popov, Irkutsk, 1962

1 ♘xd5!! exd5 2 ♕xf7+!! ♔xf7 (if *2...♔h8, 3 ♘e6!* is decisive) 3 ♗xd5+ ♔g6 (if *3... ♔f8 4 ♘e6+*) 4 f5+ ♔h5 5 ♗f3+ ♔h4 6 g3+ Black resigns. After 6...♔h3 there follows 7 ♗g2+ ♔g4 8 ♖f4+ ♔h5 9 ♗f3+ ♔h6 10 ♖h4 mate.

312. Unzicker-Antoshin, Sochi, 1965

1 ♗xf7+!! ♔xf7 2 ♕d5+ ♔f8 3 ♗d6+ ♖e7 (if *3...♗e7 4 ♖xe7! ♖xe7 5 ♕e6!*) 4 ♖e6! ♖d8 (White was threatening not only *5 ♖xf6+ gxf6 6 ♕e6*, but also *5 ♗xe7+* and *6 ♖xb6*; on *4... ♕a7* there follows *5 ♖ce1 ♖cc7 6 ♖xf6+ gxf6 7 ♕e6!!*) 5 ♗xe7+ ♗xe7 6 ♖xb6 ♖xd5 7 ♖xb2 Black resigns.

313. White to play (15 mins.)

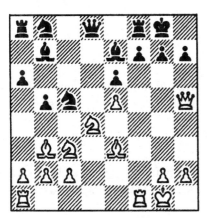

314. White to play (15 mins.)

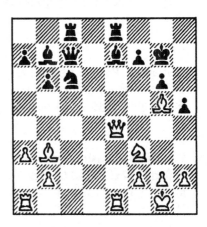

315. White to play (15 mins.)

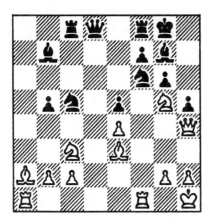

316. White to play (10 mins.)

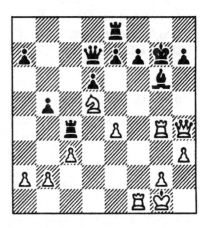

317. Black to play (12 mins.)

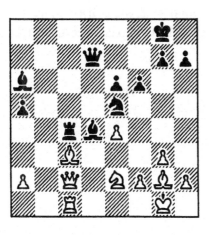

318. Black to play (12 mins.)

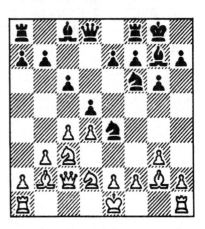

SOLUTIONS TO POSITIONS 313-318

313. Bednarski-Pytel, Lublin, 1972
1 ♖xf7!! ♖xf7 2 ♘xe6 ♘xb3 (on *2... ♕e8* there follows *3 ♘xc5 ♗xc5 4 ♖f1!*) 3 ♘xd8 g6 4 ♕d1 ♘xa1 5 ♘xb7 ♘c6 6 ♘d6 ♖d8 7 ♗b6 Black resigns.

314. Petrosian-Balashov, Moscow, 1974
1 ♗xf7! ♔xf7 2 ♗h6! ♕d6 (other moves similarly fail to prevent a check on the a2-g8 diagonal) 3 ♕c4+ ♔f6 4 ♖ad1 ♘d4 5 ♕xd4+ ♕xd4 6 ♖xd4 ♖c5 7 h4 Black resigns.

315. Filipowicz-Pokojowszyk, Warsaw, 1971
1 ♘xf7!! ♖xf7 2 ♗xf7+ ♔xf7 3 ♖a7! ♕b6 (*3... ♖b8* or *3... ♖c7* is answered by *4 ♗xc5*) 4 ♘d5! ♕xa7 5 ♖xf6+ ♔g8 (capturing on f6 leads to mate) 6 ♘e7+ ♔h7 7 ♖xg6 Black resigns. On 7...♕a1+ 8 ♗g1 ♕c1 there follows 9 ♕xh5+ ♗h6 10 ♕f5 ♕f4 11 ♖xh6+.

316. Ragozin-Veresov, Moscow, 1945
1 ♖xg6+!! fxg6 2 ♖f7+!! ♔xf7 3 ♕xh7+ ♔e6 (or *3... ♔f8 4 ♘f4!*) 4 ♕xg6+ ♔e5 5 ♕g7+ ♔xe4 6 ♘f6+ exf6 7 ♕xd7 Black resigns.

317. Adorjan-Basman, Hastings 1973/74
1...♗xf2+!! 2 ♔xf2 ♕a7+ 3 ♔e1 ♘g4 4 ♘d4 ♖xd4 5 ♗xd4 ♕xd4 6 ♕c5 ♕d3! 7 ♖c2 ♘e3 8 ♖d2 ♘xg2+ White resigns.

318. Adamski-Podgayets, Varna, 1972
1... ♘xf2!! 2 ♔xf2 ♘g4+ 3 ♔f3 (or *3 ♔e1 ♘e3*) 3...♗xd4 4 ♘d1 ♘e5+ 5 ♔f4 g5+ 6 ♔xg5 ♕d6! 7 ♖f1 ♔g7! White resigns. There is no defence against 8...♕h6 mate.

319. White to play (12 mins.)

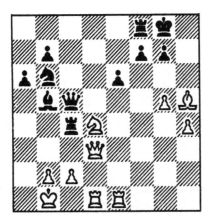

320. White to play (15 mins.)

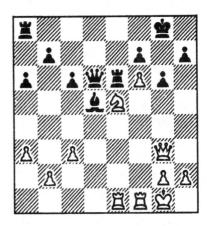

321. White to play (12 mins.)

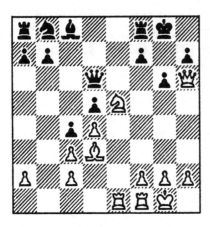

322. White to play (7 mins.)

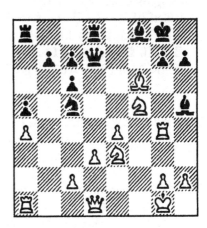

323. Black to play (12 mins.)

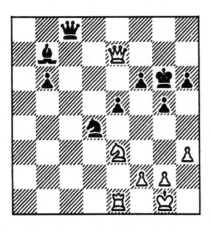

324. White to play (12 mins.)

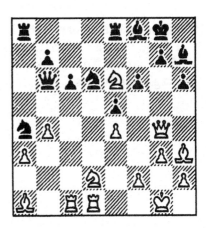

SOLUTIONS TO POSITIONS 319-324

319. Men-Yuferov, Batumi, 1972

1 ♗xf7+!! ♖xf7 (on *1...♔xf7* there follows *2 ♖f1+ ♔g8 3 ♘xe6!*) 2 ♘xe6 ♕f5 3 g6!! ♕xd3 4 gxf7+ ♔xf7 5 ♖xd3 ♖xh4 6 ♖f3+ ♔g6 7 ♖g1+ ♔h6 8 ♖f8 Black resigns.

320. Koltsov-Nikiforov, Leningrad, 1974

1 ♘xf7!! ♔xf7 (*1...♕xg3* is answered by *2 ♘h6+*) 2 ♖xe6 ♕xe6 (*2...♔xe6* loses to *3 ♖e1+ ♔d7 4 ♖e7+*) 3 ♕c7+ ♔e8 4 f7+ ♔f8 5 ♕f4 g5 6 ♕d4 ♔e7 7 ♕c5+ ♔d7 8 f8=♘+ ♖xf8 9 ♕xf8 Black resigns.

321. Krogius-Chernikov, Kuybishev, 1970

1 ♘xf7!! ♖xf7 2 ♖e8+ ♖f8 3 ♖fe1 ♘c6 4 ♗xg6! hxg6 5 ♖xf8+ ♕xf8 6 ♕xg6+ ♔h8 7 ♖e8 ♕xe8 8 ♕xe8+, and White won. The game concluded 8...♔g7 9 g4 ♖b8 10 ♕h5 ♗e6 11 f4 ♗f7 12 ♕g5+ ♔f8 13 h4 ♖e8 14 h5 ♖e7 15 f5 ♗g8 16 ♕h6+ ♔e8 17 g5 ♖d7 18 g6, and Black resigned.

322. Gipslis-Novopashin, Riga, 1954

1 ♘e7+!! ♔h8 2 ♖xg7! ♗xg7 3 ♗xg7+ ♔xg7 4 ♕xh5 ♘e6 5 ♖f1! Black resigns.

323. Razuvayev-Chistyakov, Moscow, 1969

1...♗xg2!! 2 ♖b1 (the acceptance of the sacrifice loses after either *2 ♘xg2 ♘f3+ 3 ♔f1 ♕c4+ 4 ♖e2 ♘d2+ 5 ♔e1 ♕c1* mate, or *2 ♔xg2 ♕c6+ 3 ♔g1 ♘f3+ 4 ♔f1 ♕b5+ 5 ♖e2 ♘d4*, and wins) 2...♗xh3 3 ♔h2 ♕e6 4 ♕xe6 ♗xe6 5 ♖xb6 h5, and Black won.

324. Figler-Galtsev, Corr., 1969/70

1 ♘xg7!! ♗xg7 2 ♘c4 f5 (bad is *2...♘xc4 3 ♖d7*) 3 exf5 ♗xf5 4 ♕h5 ♘xc4 5 ♗xf5 ♘e3 6 ♖d7! Black resigns. On 6...♘xf5 there follows 7 ♕xf5 ♖f8 8 ♖xg7+, and mates.

325. White to play (5 mins.)

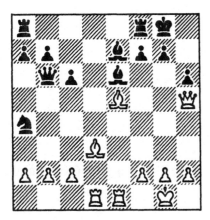

326. Black to play (12 mins.)

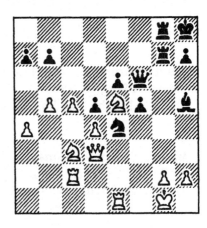

327. White to play (10 mins.)

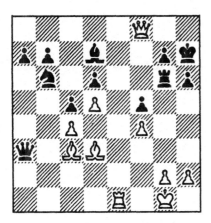

328. Black to play (8 mins.)

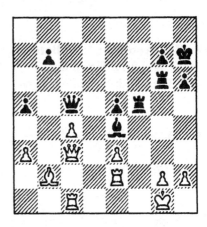

329. White to play (10 mins.)

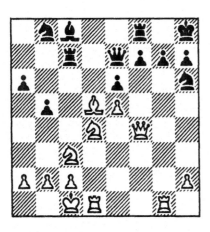

330. Black to play (12 mins.)

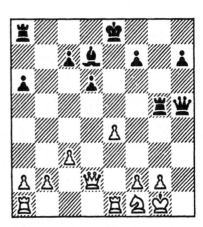

SOLUTIONS TO POSITIONS 325-330

325. Taflan-Ruzu, Bucharest, 1957
1 ♗xg7!! ♔xg7 2 ♖xe6! ♗g5 (*2...fxe6 3 ♕g6+ ♔h8 4 ♕h7 mate*) 3 ♖g6+! ♔h8 4 ♖xh6+! ♗xh6 5 ♕xh6+ ♔g8 6 ♕h7 mate.

326. Bitman-Solovyev, Dubna, 1969
1... ♖xg2+!! 2 ♖xg2 ♖xg2+ 3 ♔xg2 ♕g5+ 4 ♔f1 ♕f4+ 5 ♘f3 ♗xf3 6 ♕e3 ♕xh2 7 ♖e2 ♕h3+ White resigns.

327. Gligoric-Hort, Moscow, 1963
1 ♗xg7!! ♖xg7 2 ♗xf5+ ♗xf5 3 ♕xf5+ ♖g6 (if *3...♔h8 4 ♖e8+ ♖g8 5 ♕f6+ ♔h7 6 ♖e7+*) 4 ♖e7+ ♔h8 5 ♕f8+ ♖g8 6 ♕xh6 mate.

328. Zita-Antoshin, Ulan Bator, 1965
1...♗xg2!! 2 ♖xg2 ♖xg2+ 3 ♔xg2 ♕c6+ 4 e4 ♕xe4+ 5 ♔g1 ♖g5+ 6 ♔f1 ♕h1+ 7 ♔e2 ♕xh2+ White resigns.

329. Zaitsev,I-Makarov, Moscow, 1955
1 ♖xg7!! ♔xg7 2 ♖g1+ ♔h8 3 ♕xh6 f6 4 ♘f5! exf5 5 exf6 ♕d8 (if *5...♕xf6 6 ♕xf6+ ♖xf6 7 ♖g8 mate*) 6 ♕g7+ ♖xg7 7 fxg7 mate.

330. Rappaz-Leresh, Lozanna, 1974
1... ♖xg2+!! 2 ♔xg2 ♗h3+ 3 ♔h2 ♗g4+ 4 ♔g3 (or *4 ♔g1 ♗f3!*) 4...♕h3+ 5 ♔f4 ♕f3+ 6 ♔g5 ♗e7! 7 ♕e3 ♖g8+ 8 ♔h4 ♕f6+ 9 ♔g3 ♗e6+ White resigns.

331. Black to play (14 mins.)

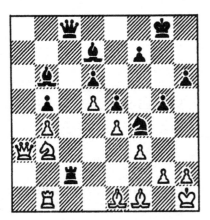

332. Black to play (16 mins.)

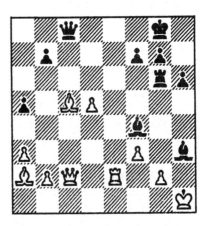

333. White to play (20 mins.)

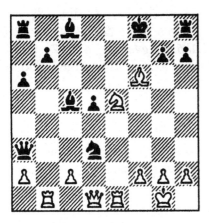

334. White to play (15 mins.)

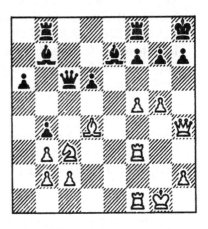

335. White to play (25 mins.)

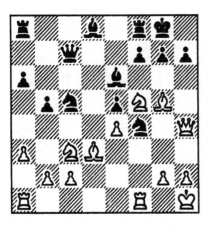

336. White to play (15 mins.)

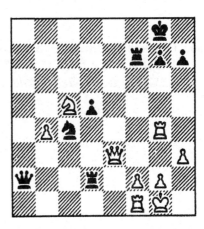

SOLUTIONS TO POSITIONS 331-336

331. Bikov-Chubukov, Tomsk, 1970
1...♖xg2!! *(1... ♘xg2 2 ♗xg2 ♗h3* fails to win after *3 ♘d2!)* 2 ♗xg2 ♗h3! 3 ♖b2 ♗xg2+ 4 ♖xg2 ♕h3 5 ♕b2 ♕xf3 6 ♘c5 dxc5 7 ♗g3 c4 8 h3 ♕f1+ White resigns *(9 ♔h2 ♗g1+* leads to mate).

332. Gufeld-Shereshevsky, Tbilisi, 1973
1...♗xg2+! 2 ♖xg2 ♕h3+ 3 ♔g1 ♗h2+ 4 ♔f1 (or *4 ♔h1 ♗d6+ 5 ♔g1 ♗xc5+)* 4...♕xf3+ 5 ♕f2 *(5 ♖f2 ♖g1* mate) 5...♕d1+ 6 ♕e1 ♕xe1+ 7 ♔xe1 ♖xg2 8 d6 ♖xb2 9 d7 ♗c7 10 ♗d6 ♗d8 11 ♗c4 b5 White resigns.

333. Reshevsky-Vasconcellos, Boston, 1944
1 ♗xg7+!! ♔xg7 2 ♖xb7+! ♗e7 *(2...♗xb7* loses after *3 ♕g4+ ♔f6 4 ♕f3+ ♔g7 -* 4...♔e7 5 ♕f7+ ♔d6 6 ♕d7* mate - *5 ♕f7+ ♔h6 6 ♕f6+ ♔h5 7 g4* mate) 3 ♕h5! ♖f8 (here too *3...♗xb7* loses after *4 ♕f7+ ♔h6 5 ♘g4+ ♔g5 6 ♕g7+ ♔f5 7 ♘h6+ ♔f4 8 ♕g3* mate) 4 ♕g5+ ♔h8 5 ♘g6+! hxg6 6 ♕h6+ ♔g8 7 ♕xg6+ ♔h8 8 ♖bxe7 Black resigns.

334. Fischer-Cardoso, New York, 1957
1 ♗xg7+!! ♔xg7 2 ♕h6+ ♔h8 3 g6! ♕c5+ 4 ♖1f2 fxg6 5 fxg6 ♕g5+ 6 ♕xg5 ♗xg5 7 ♖xf8+ ♖xf8 8 ♖xf8+ ♔g7 9 gxh7 Black resigns.

335. Ravinsky-Ilivitsky, Riga, 1951
1 ♘xg7!! ♔xg7 *(1... ♘cxd3 2 ♕g3!!)* 2 ♖xf4!! exf4 3 ♕h6+ ♔g8 4 ♗f6! ♗xf6 5 e5!! ♘xd3 6 exf6 ♘f2+ 7 ♔g1 ♘h3+ 8 ♔f1 ♗c4+ 9 ♘e2 Black resigns *(9...♗xe2+ 10 ♔e1).*

336. Gligoric-Gudmundsson, Amsterdam, 1951 (variation)
1 ♕e8+ ♖f8 2 ♖xg7+! ♔xg7 3 ♕e7+ ♖f7 (or *3... ♔g8 4 ♘e6)* 4 ♕g5+ ♔h8 (if *4... ♔f8 5 ♘e6+ ♔e8 6 ♕d8* mate) 5 ♕d8+ ♔g7 6 ♘e6+ ♔g6 7 ♕g5 mate.

337. White to play (20 mins.)

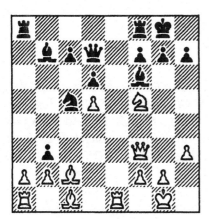

338. White to play (12 mins.)

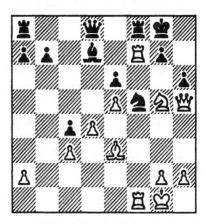

339. White to play (20 mins.)

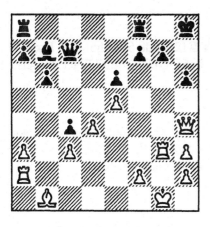

340. White to play (10 mins.)

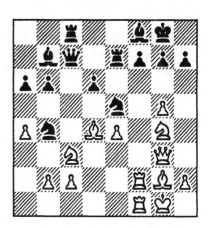

341. White to play (10 mins.)

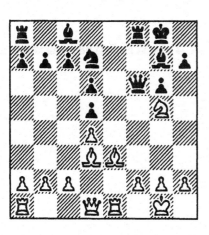

342. White to play (12 mins.)

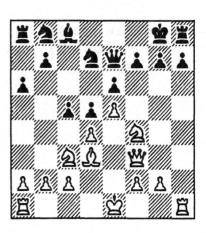

SOLUTIONS TO POSITIONS 337-342

337. Pilan-Minsker, Tel Aviv, 1966

1 ♘xg7! ♔xg7 (the alternatives were *1...♔xg7 2 ♗h6+ ♔xh6 3 ♕xf6+ ♔h5 4 ♗d1+*, *1...bxc2 2 ♕xf6 ♖d8 3 ♖e7 ♘e4 4 ♕h4 ♗xd5 5 ♘f5 ♖h8 6 ♗g5*, or *1... ♖xa2 2 ♕xf6 ♖xa1 3 ♘f5*) 2 ♗f5! ♖d8 3 ♕h5 h6 4 ♗xh6 ♕f6 5 ♗xg7 ♕xg7 6 ♖e3! ♖xa2 7 ♖ae1! Black resigns. A possible finish is 7...♗c8 8 ♖g3 ♗xf5 9 ♖xg7+ ♔xg7 10 ♕xf5 ♖xb2 11 ♖e3 f6 12 ♖g3+ ♔f7 13 ♕h7+ ♔e8 14 ♖e3+ ♔d8 15 ♕e7+.

338. Miguel-Sanguinetti, Parana, 1950

1 ♖1xf5!! exf5 2 ♖xg7+! ♔xg7 3 ♘e6+ ♗xe6 4 ♗xh6+ ♔h7 5 ♗g5+ ♔g7 6 ♕h6+ ♔f7 7 ♗xd8 ♖axd8 8 ♕f6+ ♔g8 9 ♕xe6+ ♔g7 10 ♕e7+ Black resigns.

339. Szabo-Pogats, Budapest, 1954

1 ♖xg7!! ♔xg7 2 ♕f6+ ♔g8 3 f3! ♗xf3 4 ♖f2! ♕d8 5 ♕xh6! f5 6 ♖xf3 ♔f7 7 ♖g3 ♕d5 8 ♖g7+ ♔e8 9 ♕g6+ ♔d8 10 ♕g5+ ♔c8 11 ♕e7 Black resigns.

340. Smyslov-Hort, Petropolis, 1973

1 ♗xe5! dxe5 2 ♘f6+! ♔h8 3 ♘xh7!! ♖e6 (*3... ♔xh7 would have been answered by 4 g6+! fxg6 5 ♖xf8, with a mating attack*) 4 ♖xf7 ♗c5+ (*if 4... ♕c5+ 5 ♔h1 ♔xh7 6 ♕h3+ and 7 ♕xe6*) 5 ♔h1 ♖e7 6 ♖f8+! Black resigns.

341. Todorcevic-Jine, France, 1969

1 ♘xh7!! ♔xh7 2 ♕h5+ ♔g8 3 ♗xg6 ♖f7 4 ♕h7+ ♔f8 5 ♗h6!! ♗xh6 6 ♕xh6+ ♕g7 7 ♖e8+!! Black resigns.

342. Keres-Wade, London, 1954

1 ♗xh7+! ♖xh7 2 ♖xh7 ♔xh7 3 0-0-0! f5 4 ♖h1+ ♔g8 5 ♖h8+!! ♔xh8 6 ♘g6+ Black resigns.

343. White to play (8 mins.)

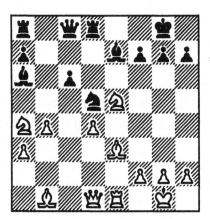

344. White to play (16 mins.)

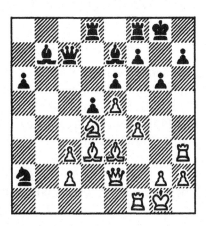

345. White to play (15 mins.)

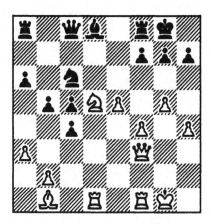

346. White to play (15 mins.)

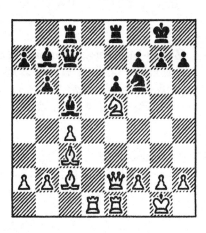

347. White to play (15 mins.)

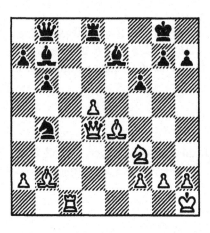

348. Black to play (12 mins.)

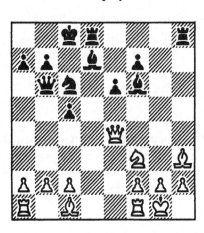

SOLUTIONS TO POSITIONS 343-348

343. Kracunov-Kirov, Tirnovo, 1963

1 ♗xh7+!! ♔xh7 (on *1... ♔f8* there follows *2 ♕h5 g6 3 ♗h6+ ♔e8 4 ♕xg6!!*, while *2... ♕e6* is no better in view of *3 ♗f5!*) 2 ♕h5+ ♔g8 3 ♕xf7+ ♔h7 4 ♗h6!! ♗f6 (*4... ♔xh6 5 ♕g6* mate, or *4... ♖g8 5 ♕g6+ ♔h8 6 ♘f7* mate) 5 ♗xg7! ♗xg7 6 ♖e4! Black resigns.

344. Klovan-Olifer, Yaroslavl, 1966

1 ♖xh7!! ♗c8 (or *1... ♔xh7 2 ♕h5+ ♔g8 - 2...♔g7 3 ♘xe6+! - 3 ♗xg6! fxg6 4 ♕xg6+ ♔h8 5 ♘xe6*, and wins) 2 ♖h6 ♔g7 3 ♕g4! ♖h8 (bad is *3... ♔xh6 4 f5+ ♔g7 5 f6+ ♔g8 6 ♗xg6*) 4 ♖xg6+!! ♔f8 (or *4...fxg6 5 ♕xg6+! ♔f8 6 f5!*) 5 f5! exf5 (after *5...fxg6 6 fxe6+* White wins) 6 ♖g8+!! Black resigns. On 6... ♖xg8 comes 7 ♗h6+ ♔e8 8 ♕xg8+ ♔d7 9 ♗xf5 mate.

345. Zwaig-Martinez, Havana, 1966

1 ♗xh7+! ♔xh7 2 ♘f6+! ♗xf6 (or *2...gxf6 3 ♕h5+ and 4 gxf6*) 3 ♕h5+ ♔g8 4 gxf6 ♘xe5 (*4... ♘d8 5 ♖xd8* is no better) 5 fxe5 ♕e6 6 ♕g5 g6 7 ♕h6, and White won. The finish was 7...♕g4+ 8 ♔h2 ♕e2+ 9 ♔h3, and Black resigned.

346. Kots-Riskin, Sverdlovsk, 1963

1 ♗xh7+!! ♔xh7 (*1... ♘xh7* is answered by *2 ♖d7 ♕b8 3 ♖xf7 ♘f6 4 ♖xf6! and 5 ♕g4+*, while if *3...♗f8 4 ♕h5!* followed by *5 ♖e3*, and wins) 2 ♖d7!! ♘xd7 (forced, since *3 ♖xf7* was threatened, while *2... ♕b8* fails to *3 ♖xf7 ♗c7 4 ♕d3+ and 5 ♕g6!*) 3 ♕h5+ ♔g8 4 ♕xf7+ ♔h7 5 ♘xd7 ♕xd7 (or *5... ♖g8 6 ♘f6+ and 7 ♕h5* mate) 6 ♕xd7 ♖e7 7 ♕d3+ ♔g8 8 b4 Black resigns.

347. Barcza-Golombek, Stockholm, 1952

1 ♗xh7+! ♔xh7 2 ♕e4+ ♔g8 (on *2... ♔h8* there follows *3 ♘g5 fxg5 4 ♕xe7 ♖g8 5 ♕xg5*) 3 ♕xe7 ♘xd5 4 ♕e6+ ♔h8 (if *4... ♔h7 5 ♕f5+ g6 6 ♕h3+ ♔g8 7 ♘g5!! fxg5 8 ♖e1!*) 5 ♕h3+ ♔g8 6 ♘g5! fxg5 7 ♕e6+ Black resigns. On 7...♔h7 there follows 8 ♕f7 ♖g8 9 ♕h5 mate.

348. Zuckerman-Fedin, Moscow, 1973

1...♖xh3!! 2 gxh3 ♖g8+ 3 ♔h1 ♘d4! 4 ♘xd4 ♗xd4 5 f3 ♗c6 6 ♕e2 ♕b5! White resigns. Since if 7 c4 ♕xc4! 8 ♕xc4 ♗xf3+ 9 ♖xf3 ♖g1 mate, or 7 ♕d1 ♕xf1+! 8 ♕xf1 ♗xf3+ 9 ♕xf3 ♖g1 mate.

349. White to play (10 mins.)

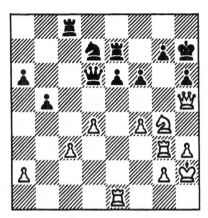

350. White to play (12 mins.)

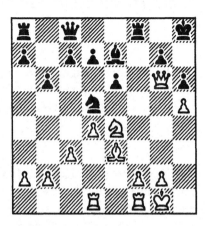

351. White to play (15 mins.)

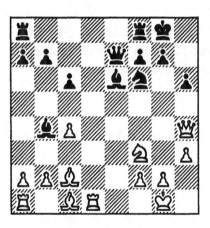

352. White to play (10 mins.)

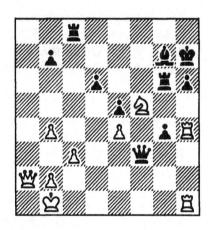

353. White to play (15 mins.)

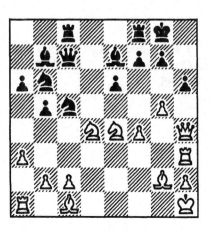

354. White to play (20 mins.)

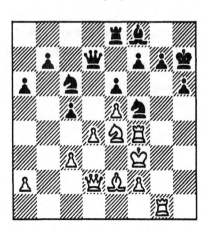

SOLUTIONS TO POSITIONS 349-354

349. Tolush-Bannik, Riga, 1958
1 ♘xh6! gxh6 2 ♖xe6! ♕xe6 (or *2... ♖xe6 3 ♕g6+ ♔h8 4 ♕xh6* mate) 3 ♖g6
♔h8 4 ♖xh6+ ♔g7 (if *4... ♔g8 5 ♖h8+ ♔g7 6 ♕h7* mate) 5 ♕g6+ ♔f8 6 ♖h8+
Black resigns.

350. Gligoric-Prins, Stockholm, 1952
1 ♗xh6!! gxh6 2 ♕xh6+ ♔g8 3 ♖d3 ♗h4 4 ♖g3+! ♗xg3 (on *4... ♔f7* there follows *5 ♖f3+ ♔g8* - or 5...♔e7 *6 ♕g7+*, and mate in two moves - *6 ♘g5! ♗xg5 7*
♕xg5+ ♔h7 8 ♕g6+ ♔h8 9 ♖g3, with inevitable mate) 5 ♕g6+ ♔h8 6 ♘g5
Black resigns.

351. Krapfenbauer-Kalivoda, Corr., 1951
1 ♗xh6!! gxh6 (or *1...♕c5 2 ♗xg7! ♔xg7 3 ♖d5! cxd5 4 ♕g5+ ♔h8 5 ♕xf6+*
♔g8 6 ♕g5+ ♔h8 7 ♕h6+ ♔g8 8 ♕h7 mate) 2 ♕xh6 ♖fd8 (or *2...♕xc4 3 ♖d4*)
3 ♘g5 ♗c5 4 ♗h7+ ♔h8 5 ♗f5+ ♔g8 6 ♘e4!! Black resigns.

352. Kanyumov-Barenbaum, Alma-Ata, 1971
1 ♖xh6+!! ♖xh6 2 ♖xh6+ ♗xh6 3 ♕f7+ ♔h8 4 ♕f6+ ♔g8 5 ♘e7+ ♔h7 6
♕g6+ ♔h8 7 ♕xh6 mate.

353. Newman-Franklin, London, 1953
1 ♘f6+!! ♔h8 (*1...gxf6 2 ♕xh6* and *3 ♕h8* mate, or *1...♗xf6 2 gxf6* followed by *3*
fxg7 and *4 ♕xh6*) 2 ♕xh6+!! gxh6 3 ♖xh6+ ♔g7 4 ♖h7+ ♔g6 5 f5+! exf5 6
♖h6+ ♔g7 7 ♘xf5 mate.

354. Rossolimo-N.N., Paris, 1944
1 ♖xf5!! exf5 2 ♕xh6+!! ♔xh6 (or *2...gxh6 3 ♘f6+* and *4 ♖g8* mate) 3 ♖h1+
♔g6 4 ♔f4!! (threatening *5 ♗h5+* and *6 ♗xf7* mate) 4...♕e6 5 ♖h8!! Black
resigns. There is no defence against mate by 6 ♗h5.

355. White to play (7 mins.)

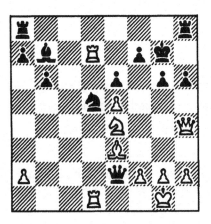

356. White to play (12 mins.)

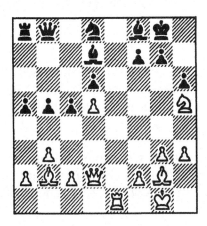

357. White to play (12 mins.)

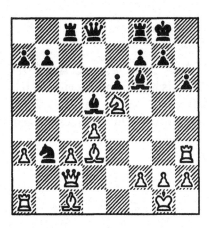

358. White to play (20 mins.)

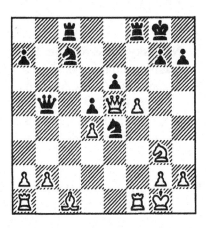

359. White to play (16 mins.)

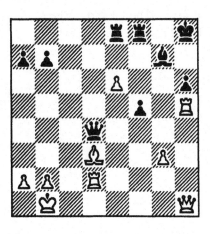

360. White to play (18 mins.)

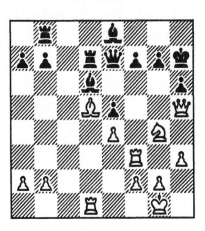

SOLUTIONS TO POSITIONS 355-360

355. Cortlever-Donner, Beverwijk, 1950 (variation)
1 ♗xh6+!! ♖xh6 2 ♕f6+!! ♘xf6 3 exf6+ ♔h7 4 ♘g5+ ♔h8 5 ♖d8+ ♖xd8 6 ♖xd8 mate. White in fact overlooked this possibility, and the game ended in a draw.

356. Spassky-Kholmov, Rostov, 1971
1 ♕xh6!! gxh6 (forced, since *2 ♘f6+!* was threatened) 2 ♘f6+ ♔h8 3 ♘xd7+ ♔g8 (if *3... ♔h7 4 ♘xf8+ and 5 ♘d7*) 4 ♖e8! ♘c6 5 dxc6 ♕a7 6 c7 Black resigns.

357. Bronstein,I-Bobovnikov, Liepaja, 1970
1 ♗h7+ ♔h8 2 ♗xh6! gxh6 3 ♖xh6 ♔g7 4 ♗g8! ♔xh6 5 ♕h7+ ♔g5 6 h4+ ♔f4 7 g3 mate.

358. Nicevsky-Ioffe, Skopje, 1969
1 ♗h6 gxh6 (forced, since if *1... ♘f6 2 ♗xg7 ♔xg7 3 ♘h5+*, or *1... ♘f6 2 fxe6 ♖xh6 3 ♘f5!*) 2 fxe6! ♕e8 (the threat of *3 ♘h5!* is highly unpleasant, and if *2... ♖xf1+ 3 ♖xf1 ♕e8*, then *4 ♘h5!* is decisive) 3 e7! ♖xf1+ (or *3... ♖f7 4 ♖xf7 ♕xf7 5 ♖f1!*) 4 ♖xf1 ♕g6 5 ♘xe4 ♕xe4 (on *5...dxe4* White decides the game by *6 d5* and *7 d6*) 6 ♖f8+! ♖xf8 7 ♕h8+!! Black resigns.

359. Kristiansen-Moe, Denmark, 1973
1 ♖xh6+! ♗xh6 2 ♕xh6+ ♔g8 3 ♗c4! ♕g1+ (or *3... ♕e4+ 4 ♖c2*) 4 ♔c2 ♖c8 5 ♕g6+ ♔h8 6 ♕h5+ ♔g8 7 ♕g5+ ♔h8 8 ♕h4+ Black resigns (*8...♔g8 9 e7+!*).

360. Addison-Evans, New York, 1966
1 ♖f6!! ♕f8 2 ♖xh6+! gxh6 3 ♘f6+ ♔g7 4 ♕f5! ♖bd8 5 ♖d3 ♕h8 6 ♖g3+ ♔f8 7 ♘h7+ ♔e7 8 ♖g8!! ♕xh7 9 ♕xh7 Black resigns.

361. White to play (20 mins.)

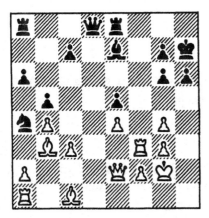

362. White to play (20 mins.)

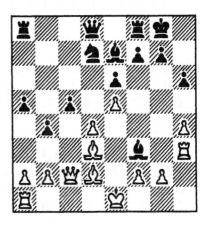

363. White to play (15 mins.)

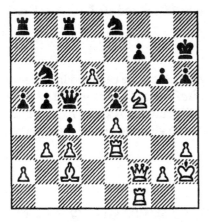

364. White to play (12 mins.)

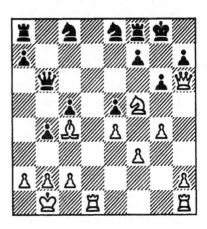

365. White to play (8 mins.)

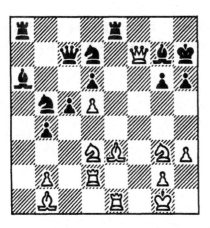

366. White to play (12 mins.)

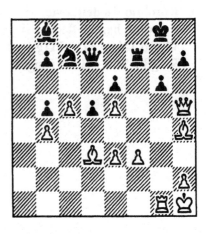

SOLUTIONS TO POSITIONS 361-366

361. Gurgenidze-Klovan, Yerevan, 1959
1 ♗xh6!! gxh6 (if *1...♔xh6 2 ♖h1+*) 2 ♖d1! ♕c8 3 ♖f7+ ♔h8 4 ♕e3 ♗g5 5 ♕xg5!! hxg5 6 ♖h1+ ♔g8 7 ♖d7+ Black resigns.

362. Portisch-Johannessen, Havana, 1966
1 ♗xh6!! ♗xh4 (on *1...gxh6* there follows *2 ♖g3+ ♔h8 3 ♕d2 ♗g5 4 hxg5 h5 5 g6! ♔g7 6 gxf7+ ♔xf7 7 ♕h6*) 2 gxf3 gxh6 3 ♘e2 ♘xe5 4 dxe5 ♕d4 5 ♖xh4! ♕xh4 6 ♖g1+ ♔h8 7 ♕c1! f6 8 ♖g6! Black resigns.

363. Goikhman-Figler, Kishinyov, 1975
1 ♘xh6!! ♔xh6 2 ♕h4+ ♔g7 3 ♖xf7+!! ♔xf7 4 ♕h7+ ♘g7 5 ♖f3+ ♔e8 6 ♕xg6+ ♔d7 7 ♖f7+ ♔c6 8 d7+! ♕d6 9 dxc8=♕+ ♘xc8 10 ♖f6! Black resigns.

364. Platonov-Savon, Odessa, 1968
1 ♖d6!! ♕c7 (an extraordinary position! - the rook can be captured in three ways, but they all lead to catastrophe: *1...♘cxd6 2 ♘e7 mate*, *1...♘exd6 2 ♕g7 mate*, or *1...♕xd6 2 ♘xd6*, when White wins without difficulty) 2 ♖xg6+! hxg6 3 ♕xg6+ ♔h8 4 ♕h6+ ♔g8 5 g5! Black resigns. Against 6 g6, followed by mate, there is no defence.

365. Marmagen-Kiune, Corr., 1966
1 ♕xg6+!! ♔xg6 (*1...♔h8 2 ♘e5!*, or *1...♔g8 2 ♘f5!*) 2 ♘e5+ ♔f6 3 ♖f2+ ♔e7 (or *3...♔xe5 4 ♖f5 mate*) 4 ♘c6+ ♕xc6 5 ♗g5 mate.

366. Korchnoi-Nedeljkovic, Vienna, 1957
1 ♗xg6!! hxg6 2 ♖xg6+ ♔g7 3 ♗f6! ♘e8 (or *3...♖xg6 4 ♕xg6+ ♔f8 5 ♕h6+ ♔g8 6 ♕h8+ ♔f7 7 ♕g7+ ♔e8 8 ♕g8 mate*) 4 ♖h6 ♔f8 5 ♖h8+ ♖g8 6 ♖xg8+ ♔xg8 7 ♕h8+ Black resigns.

367. White to play (16 mins.)

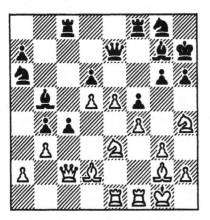

368. White to play (20 mins.)

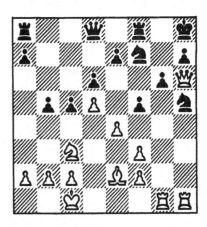

369. White to play (10 mins.)

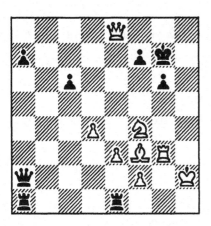

370. White to play (15 mins.)

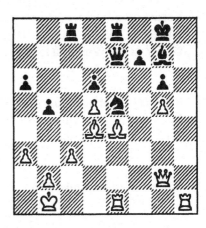

371. Black to play (10 mins.)

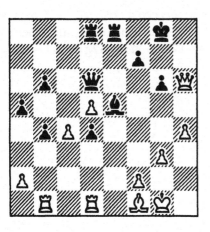

372. White to play (20 mins.)

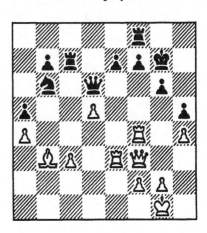

SOLUTIONS TO POSITIONS 367-372

367. Zelinsky-Skotorenko, Corr., 1973/74
1 ♘xg6! ♔xg6 2 ♘xf5! ♖xf5 3 ♕xf5+!! ♔xf5 4 ♗e4+ ♔g4 5 h3+ ♔xg3 (no better is *5...♔xh3 6 ♗f5+ ♔xg3 7 ♖e3+ ♔h4 8 ♖h3 mate*, or *5...♔h5 6 g4+ ♔h4 7 ♖e3 and 8 ♗e1 mate*) 6 ♖e3+ ♔h4 7 ♗g6!! Black resigns. 7...♕g5+ does not help after 8 fxg5 ♗xe5 9 ♖e4+ ♔xh3 10 ♗f5+ ♔g3 11 ♗e1 mate.

368. Planinc-Marangunic, Novi Travnik, 1969
1 ♕xg6!! hxg6 2 ♖xg6 ♘h6 3 ♖xh5 ♖f7 4 ♖gxh6+ ♔g7 5 ♖h7+ ♔g8 6 ♖h8+ ♔g7 7 ♖5h7+ ♔g6 8 exf5+ ♖xf5 9 ♖xd8 ♖xd8 10 ♗d3 ♔xh7 11 ♗xf5+ ♔h6 12 ♘xb5, and White won.

369. Koraskov-Khasin, Kishinyov, 1950
1 ♖xg6+!! fxg6 2 ♘e6+ ♔f6 3 ♕f8+! ♔xe6 4 ♗g4+ ♔d5 5 ♕f7+ ♔e4 6 ♕xg6+ ♔d5 7 ♕f7+ ♔e4 8 ♕f5 mate.

370. Khavsky-Zhelyandinov, Sevastopol, 1970
1 ♗xg6!! fxg6 2 ♕h3 ♖f8 3 ♕h7+ ♔f7 4 ♗xe5 dxe5 5 ♖hf1+ ♔e8 6 ♕xg6+ ♖f7 7 d6! Black resigns.

371. Sliwa-Smyslov, Lodz, 1955
1...♗xg3!! 2 fxg3 ♕xg3+ 3 ♔h1 (or *3 ♗g2 ♖e2*, with inevitable mate) 3...♖e4! 4 ♖b3 ♖xh4+ 5 ♗h3 ♕xb3 6 ♕xh4 ♕xd1+ White resigns.

372. Smyslov-Liberzon, Moscow, 1969
1 ♖e6! ♕c5 2 ♖xg6+!! fxg6 (*2...♔xg6 is bad on account of 3 ♕g3+ ♔h7 4 ♖f5 ♖c6 5 ♗c2! ♖g6 6 ♖xf7+!*) 3 ♖xf8 ♕xc3 (*3...♖c8 is no better, since there follows 4 ♖f7+ ♔h8 5 ♕f4 ♔g8 6 d6!*) 4 ♕f7+ ♔h6 5 ♕f4+ ♔g7 6 ♖f7+ ♔g8 7 d6! ♕xb3 8 ♖f8+ Black resigns.

373. White to play (20 mins.)

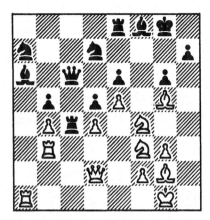

374. Black to play (25 mins.)

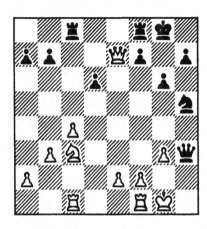

375. White to play (15 mins.)

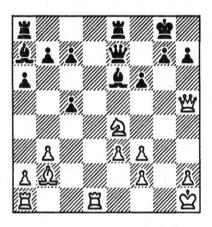

376. Black to play (25 mins.)

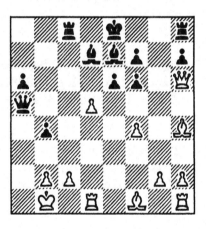

377. Black to play (20 mins.)

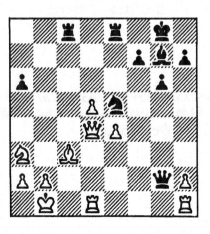

378. Black to play (15 mins.)

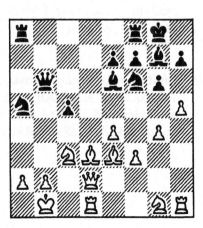

SOLUTIONS TO POSITIONS 373-378

373. Bokuchava-Georgadze, Tbilisi, 1970
1 ♘xg6!! hxg6 2 ♕d3 ♗g7 (*2... ♔g7* is answered by *3 ♘h4!*) 3 ♖xa6!! ♕xa6 4 ♕xg6 ♘f8 (no better is *4... ♕c8 5 ♗f6 ♘xf6 6 exf6 ♖c7 7 ♖c3!!*, or *4... ♖cc8 5 ♗f6 ♘xf6 6 exf6 ♕b7 7 ♘g5!*, and wins) 5 ♕xe8 ♕a2 6 ♘h3 ♖c6 7 ♖e3 ♕b1+ 8 ♔g2 ♕xb4 9 ♗e7 ♕c4 10 ♘xf8 Black resigns.

374. Bannik-Tal, Riga, 1955
1... ♘xg3!! 2 fxg3 ♕xg3+ 3 ♔h1 ♖ce8 4 ♕xb7 (no better is *4 ♕f6 ♖e5 5 ♕f3 ♕h4+* - but not *5... ♖h5+? 6 ♕xh5 gxh5 7 ♖g1 - 6 ♔g1 ♖g5+*) 4... ♖e5 5 ♕g2 ♖h5+ 6 ♔g1 ♕e3+ 7 ♕f2 ♕h6 (now Black threatens *8... ♖h1+ 9 ♔g2 ♕h3* mate, as well as *8... ♖g5+*) 8 ♕xa7 ♕g5+ 9 ♔f2 ♖h2+ 10 ♔e1 (if *10 ♔f3 ♖h3+ 11 ♔e4* - or *11 ♔f2 ♕g3* mate - *11... ♖c8+ 12 ♔d4 ♕e5* mate) 10... ♕xc1+ White resigns.

375. Sigurjonsson-Segal, Ibbs, 1968
1 ♘xf6+!! gxf6 2 ♖g1+ ♔h8 3 ♕h6! ♖f8 4 ♖g6! ♗f5 5 ♖xf6 ♔g8 6 ♖g1+ ♗g6 7 ♖gxg6+ hxg6 8 ♕xg6+ Black resigns.

376. Tolush-Bakulin, Kislovodsk, 1960
1... ♖xc2!! 2 ♔xc2 (forced, since *2... ♖xb2+!* was threatened) 2...b3+! 3 ♔d3 ♕xd5+ 4 ♔e2 ♕e4+ 5 ♔f2 ♗c5+ 6 ♔g3 ♖g8+ 7 ♗g5 fxg5 8 fxg5 ♕e3+ 9 ♔g4 ♖g6 10 ♕h5 f5+ 11 ♔h4 ♗e7 12 g3 ♕xg5+!! 13 ♕xg5 ♖h6 mate.

377. Alatortsev-Smyslov, Moscow, 1946
1... ♖xc3!! 2 ♕xc3 (*2 bxc3* fails to *2... ♕b8+*) 2... ♘c4! 3 ♕b4 a5 4 ♕b3 ♘xa3+ 5 bxa3 (or *5 ♕xa3 ♖b8 6 b3 ♕xe4+*) 5... ♕xe4+ 6 ♕d3 ♖b8+ 7 ♔c1 ♖c8+ 8 ♔b1 ♕e5 White resigns.

378. Chubarev-Tsarenko, Minsk, 1970
1... ♗xa2+!! 2 ♘xa2 ♘b3 3 ♕e2 ♖xa2! 4 ♔xa2 ♕a5+ 5 ♔xb3 (*5 ♔b1* is no better in view of *5... ♘d5! 6 ♔c2 ♘b4+ 7 ♔xb3 ♕a2* mate, or *6 ♗c1 ♘b4*) 5... ♖b8+ 6 ♔c2 ♖xb2+! 7 ♔xb2 ♘xe4+ 8 ♔c1 ♕a3+ 9 ♔c2 ♕b2 mate.

INDEX OF PLAYERS

Adamski 83, 318
Addison 360
Adorjan 317
Aisinger 267
Ajonen 211
Akopian 92
Alatortsev 377
Albano 151
Alburt 51
Alexander 74
Alivitra 123
Amosov 68
Andersen 140, 156
Andreyev 208
Anen 34
Antoshin 172, 196, 312, 328
Arabkertsev 42
Averbakh 120

Bachmann 46
Badenstein 249
Bagirov 147
Baikov 7
Bajec 155
Bakhtiar 71
Bakulin 21, 221, 376
Balashov 69, 281, 314
Balayev 138
Balinas 115
Banas 124
Bannik 349, 374
Baraty 88
Barcza 85, 347
Barden 231
Barenbaum 352
Barendregt 117, 206
Barnes 251
Bartrina 153
Basman 317
Batakov 217

Baum 86
Bednarski 313
Begun 208
Belic 24
Bellon 14
Bena 66
Benau 112
Benesch 99
Beni 60
Berebora 17
Bernstein 263
Berta 52
Bertok 195, 274
Beszterczei 114
Betotsky 243
Bikov 331
Bilek 78
Bitman 238, 326
Boatner 262
Bobotsov 157
Bobovnikov 357
Bobrov 237
Boey 204
Bogatirev 261
Bogkof 67
Bogoslovsky 304
Bokuchava 373
Boleslavsky 152, 303
Bonasitz 224
Booth 84
Both 84
Botterill 301
Botvinnik 168
Bouwmeester 122
Boyarinov 57
Boze 266
Bredewout 197
Bronstein 13, 253, 284
Bronstein, I 357
Brunner 62

Bubnov 23
Buturin 53
Byrne, R 46

Capelan 202
Cardoso 20, 98, 110, 334
Castanga 37
Chandler 22
Chechelian 7, 200
Chekhlov 217
Cherepkov 18, 59
Chernenko 118
Chernikov 321
Chistyakov 21, 323
Chubarev 378
Chubukov 331
Chukayev 104
Ciaceli 81
Ciocaltea 227
Ciric 234
Civic 287
Corning 180
Cortlever 355
Csom 181
Czerniak 80

Dagne 164
Damjanovic 154
Danov 144
Daskalov 276
Davey 134
de Visente 265
Debarnot 111
Dely 177, 184
Dementiev 298
Demeny 114
Denik 266
Denker 183
Diemer 90
Djindjihashvili 169
Donner 198, 355
Doronet 215
Dreskievic 242
Duke 28
Dvoiris 259
Dvoryetsky 240
Dyaltov 141

Ebralidze 1
Emelianov 261
Engels 20
Enklaar 82
Ermenkov 222
Estrin 192
Etruk 279
Euwe 166, 173
Evans 162, 360

Faibisovich 15
Farland 38
Fazekas 255
Fedin 348
Feldman 37
Ferholt 82
Fichtl 307
Figler 324, 363
Fiklni 205
Filep 199
Filip 75, 96, 204
Filipowicz 315
Fischer 334
Flohr 303
Forgacs 149
Franklin 353
Freidl 132
Fridjonsson 174
Furman 57, 165

Gakometti 308
Galik 193
Galtsev 324
Gawlikowksi 163
Geller 171
Genin 18, 130
Georgadze 373
Gerasimov 297
Gereben 226
Gergeli 287
Gheorghiu 188, 239
Ghinde 302
Ghitescu 153
Gipslis 322
Gligoric 9, 142, 239, 256, 327, 336, 350
Gogolev 241
Goikhman 363

Golan 101
Golbin 190
Golenishev 286
Golombek 347
Grabenweger 113
Graf 145
Grambczevski 199
Grozdev 95
Grulka 269
Grundinin 63
Gudmundsson 336
Gufeld 332
Guimard 212
Gulko 170
Gurgenidze 309, 361
Guss 79

Hairabedian 97
Hajtun 184, 234
Hall 41
Hamilton 36
Hansuit 62
Hartston 122
Hassani 235
Haygarth 36
Hecht 143
Hennings 288
Hernandez 61
Herzog 113, 124
Hodak 193
Hohler 80
Honfi 2, 226, 273
Horowitz 33, 183
Hort 12, 327, 340

Ilivitsky 335
Ilyazov 138
Ioffe 270, 358
Iovcic 179
Isakson 207
Ivanov 48
Ivkov 98, 119, 258

Janke 163
Janosevic 144
Jansa 126, 260
Jiffar 112

Jine 341
Johannessen 362
Johannsson 109
Johner 214
Jonsson 210
Juarez 77
Just 107

Kabes 246
Kalivoda 351
Kamishev 306
Kampfhenkel 133
Kandolin 159
Kanyumov 352
Kapengut 171
Karaklajic 197
Karasev 26, 270
Karpenko 116
Karpov 128
Kasas 111
Kashits 150
Kaufman 278
Kavalek 278
Keene 143
Keller 85
Kellerman 132
Keres 142, 272, 342
Kevorkov 72
Khanov 158
Khasin 369
Khavsky 370
Kholmov 9, 29, 209, 356
Kinmark 188
Kirov 291, 343
Kitanov 86
Kiune 365
Klaman 26, 130
Klovan 240, 279, 298, 344, 361
Kloza 268
Kneller 271
Knesevic 56
Kochiev 32
Kogan 25, 43
Koltsov 320
Komponovo 194
Kopayev 49
Kopriva 89, 246

Kopylov 6
Koraskov 369
Korchnoi 69, 115, 185, 223, 231, 366
Koshnitsky 175
Kotek 90
Kotov 29
Kots 346
Kottnauer 87
Kovacs 60, 244
Kracunov 343
Krapfenbauer 351
Krasilnikov 304
Kreichik 47
Kremenetsky 65
Krikunov 118
Kristiansen 359
Krogius 182, 321
Kroitsaller 73
Krupsky 296
Ksarko 66
Kubanek 89
Kupper 229, 233
Kupreichik 300
Kustinsson 210
Kuznetsov 228

Lahti 211
Laipold 73
Larsen 160, 162
Lavrentiev 146
Lee 216
Lein 146
Leresh 330
Levi 4
Lewi 83
Liberzon 372
Liboreito 187
Lindner 149
Link 187
Lipnitsky 137, 290
Lipsky 91
Litkevic 249
Ljubisavlevic 151
Ljubojevic 16, 198
Lokvenc 87
Lombardy 30
Lubensky 1

Lukanin 245
Lumer 34
Lundin 11, 166, 230, 293
Lutikov 154, 252, 300
Lutsenko 102

Mabbs 74
Madoni 103
Magrin 93
Makarov 329
Makogonov 186
Maksimov 70
Malcanek 148
Malev 104
Malevsky 283
Mandel 214
Manov 97
Marangunic 368
Marjanovic 218, 254
Markland 12
Marmagen 365
Marovic 126
Martinez 345
Mastilovic 24
Matsukevich 51
Matulovic 55
Matumoto 94
Mechkarov 161
Mecking 305
Medina 106
Meistr 95
Men 319
Miagmarsuren 27
Mich 99
Miguel 338
Mikenas 19, 35
Mileika 264
Minaja 103
Minev 3, 58
Minsker 337
Mista 40, 167, 268, 307
Mitin 121
Mititelu 136
Moe 359
Mohring 288
Moiseyev 238
Mokin 310

Momo 293
Morris 207
Movshovich 105
Mukhin 200
Mukhitdinov 71

Najdorf 160, 292
Navai Ali 247
Navarovszky 40
Nebilitsin 116
Nedeljkovic 366
Negeieshi 52
Nei 100
Nersisyan 65
Newman 353
Newspaper Readers 296
Nezhmetdinov 50, 286, 306, 309
Ni 225
Niicevsky 358
Nielsen 125
Nievergelt 256
Nikiforov 320
Nikitin 5
Nilsson 81
Nippgen 201
N.N. 31, 33, 47, 109, 354
Norman-Hansen 156
Novokhatsky 4
Novopashin 322

Ojanen 159
Olifer 344
Oren 125
Ormos 243
Ortega 224
Osnos 177
Ovsepian 92

Padevsky 218, 282, 291
Palatnik 284
Palmstet 133
Panchenko 32, 254
Panno 135
Paoli 50, 227, 285
Parma 223
Pasman 257
Patterson 262

Patzl 13
Pavlitzky 45
Pederson 14
Pelinkov 3
Penczak 91
Peresipkin 203
Peretz 8
Perez 258
Peshina 283
Petri 84
Petrosian 219, 248, 314
Pilan 337
Pipitone 275
Planinc 16, 30, 368
Platonov 364
Platz 107
Podgayets 44, 318
Pogats 339
Pokojowszyk 315
Polugayevsky 78
Polyakov 150
Pomar 219
Popov 311
Portisch 206, 236, 244, 362
Pozdeyev 158
Prins 189, 350
Pytel 313

Quinteros 119, 236, 299

Rabar 155
Radulov 176, 216, 234
Ragozin 316
Rantanen 61
Rappaz 330
Rashkovsky 289
Ravinsky 335
Razuvayev 323
Rech 45
Redely 88
Reicher 136
Reshevsky 94, 333
Ribli 299
Richter 215
Riskin 346
Robatsch 260
Rocha 305

Rokhlin 39
Romanishin 203
Rossetto 110, 248, 292
Rossi 275
Rossolimo 129, 354
Rozit 63
Rubinetti 277
Rudakovsky 168
Rudenko 25
Ruzu 325

Saigin 257
Sakharov 59
Salminsh 164
Salo 229
Sanakoyev 108
Sanguinetti 338
Saprokhin 42
Sapunov 157
Sarvarov 120
Saveliev 297
Savon 295, 364
Sax 222
Sazhayev 310
Scheinke 67
Schmid 233
Schwankrais 267
Segal 375
Seidman 263
Selenskikh 228
Semenyuk 191
Serbrnik 205
Sergievsky 53
Shakhov 127
Shaligram 247
Shamkovich 221
Shapiro 271
Shashin 141
Shereshevsky 332
Sherwood 180
Shestoperov 19
Shiyanovsky 290
Shmulian 245
Sidorov 137
Sigurjonsson 131, 375
Sinev 27
Skotorenko 367

Sliwa 178, 371
Smejkal 106
Smyslov 93, 165, 173, 186, 212, 277, 340,
    371, 372, 377
Sokolov 225
Sokolsky 43
Solovyev 326
Somogyi 17
Soultanbiev 189
Spassky 202, 259, 289, 356
Spiers 134
Spiridonov 182
Sprengler 250
Steczkowski 269
Stein 276
Steiner 139, 230
Stepak 232
Sterner 152
Stiv 101
Stoltz 178
Suetin 147
Suni 123
Suttles 54
Sveshnikov 48
Szabadi 2
Szabo 5, 185, 209, 272, 273, 274, 282, 285,
    294, 339
Szeles 9
Szilagyi 117
Szmetan 77

Taflan 325
Tal 22, 31, 54, 196, 374
Tanin 70
Tarasov 72
Taskayev 76
Telman 280
Terpugov 23
Teschner 148
Thompson 251
Tiberger 242
Tilet 308
Tinworth 38
Todorcevic 341
Tolush 6, 35, 172, 195, 349, 376
Torre 176
Tribushevsky 105

Tringov 55
Troianescu 294
Troinov 311
Tsaaarenko 378
Tseitlin 10, 170, 281
Tseshkovsky 10, 191
Tukmakov 79, 135, 169, 253
Turukin 121

Ubranek 75
Uhlmann 96
Uhlrich 250
Uitumen 56
Unzicker 312
Urzica 302
Utkin 68

Vaganian 301
Vaier 140
Vardanian 102
Varshavsky 241
Vasconcellos 333
Velimirovic 174, 181
Veresov 316
Verk 264
Vetemaa 190
Vikman 179
Vitolinsh 280
Vizantiades 131
Vladimirov 64
Vorotnikov 15, 64
Vranek 167

Wade 342

Weiss 194
Weller 41
Werhegen 201
Werle 11
White 28
Wolfer 175
Wolfiner 232
Wood 129
Wurm 145

Yasvoin 49
Yuferov 319
Yusupov 237

Zabaleta 265
Zagorovsky 108
Zaitsev 39
Zaitsev, A 252
Zaitsev, I 295, 329
Zamykhovsky 213
Zapletal 192
Zayats 76
Zeinaly 100
Zelinsky 220, 367
Zgurev 161
Zhelyandinov 127, 370
Zhukovitsky 139
Zhuravlyov 44, 220
Zinn 58
Zita 328
Zsoldos 128
Zuckerman 348
Zurakhov 213
Zwaig 345